The Book of ANSWERS

The New York Public Library
Telephone Reference Service's Most
Unusual and Entertaining Questions

BARBARA BERLINER

with MELINDA COREY

and GEORGE OCHOA

A Stonesong Press Book developed with
the Telephone Reference Service,
Mid-Manhattan Library, The Branch
Libraries, The New York Public Library

BARNES
&NOBLE
BOOKS
NEW YORK

Contents

◆ ◆ ◆

Introduction v

1. American History 1
2. American Statistics 15
3. The Animal World 23
4. Crime and Criminals 35
5. The English Language 47
6. Fine Arts 63
7. The First 70
8. Geography 79
9. Holidays 91
10. The Human Body 97
11. Inventions 103
12. Library Omnibus 110
13. Literature 121
14. Myth and Folklore 134
15. New York City History 146

16. Popular Culture   154
17. The Question and Answer Hall
    of Fame   173
18. Religion   183
19. Royalty and World Leaders   194
20. Science   202
21. Sports   218
22. Trademarks   232
23. U.S. Presidents   245
24. Who Was Who   254
25. World Cultures   267
26. World History   277
27. Twelve Trick Questions and
    Popular Delusions   290

    Index   295

Introduction

◆ ◆ ◆

The Book of Answers is the product of 6.2 million questions. That is the approximate number of questions asked of the New York Public Library Telephone Reference Service over its more than two decades of existence. Every ten seconds, eight or nine hours a day, six days a week, callers from across the globe pose questions about every subject from art to zoology. How does one join the French Foreign Legion? Who were Zeus's parents? What is a "best boy"? How do you tell the sex of a cat? What are the names of the Seven Dwarfs? How big is a hockey puck? Where is Tipperary?

These are the questions to which people want to know, once knew, or think they know the answers—and they are fielded every day by the Telephone Reference Service (Tel Ref). When this central "ready reference" division opened in 1968, one person fielded all the calls. Since then, the Tel Ref staff has expanded to 10, ensconced in a 25-by-30-foot room on the second floor of the New York Public Library's Mid-Manhattan Branch. The Telephone Reference Service is the New York Public Library's front line, disseminating information about the Library (the nation's most widely used reference center) and providing quick answers in nearly every category of knowledge.

Barbara Berliner, director of the Reference Service, oversees the staff and trains new librarians in the Tel Ref routine. The routine goes like this: The phone rings and a caller asks a question, "What was Geronimo's real name?" As long as the question—like this one—does not require a medical or legal opinion, does not take more than five minutes to answer, and is not a contest, crossword puzzle, or homework query, it is fair game.

The librarian turns to one or more of the 1,800 volumes on the Reference Room's shelves. There are the staple texts—encyclopedias, dictionaries, and almanacs. There are also computer databases, a bulletin board for clippings, and a binder of articles on New York City history. There are 12 years of *Who's Who in America*, 13 AAA travel guides, five books on etiquette, and *All About Tropical Fish*. Many of the books in the Telephone Reference Room have been "Tel Refized"—pages stuffed with newspaper clippings and margins crowded with red-penciled notes concerning death dates, pseudonyms, and names of lovers.

Fortunately, the Geronimo question can be answered in Volume 4 of the *Encyclopaedia Britannica*. The librarian gets back on the phone with the Apache leader's tribal name (Goyathlay, meaning "One Who Yawns") and is ready for another call.

On any given day, the most popular question is "What are the Library's hours?" The second most popular question is whatever is needed to win a prize from a local radio station (since this violates the "no contests" rule, the librarians decline to answer once they catch on). But most of the questions are unpredictable, changing from day to day. The reasons for calling are just as varied.

Many people call strictly on business. Authors need to fill gaps in their research (What year was the Great Fire of London?); secretaries have grammatical questions (When should you use *ensure* instead of *insure*?); copy editors want to check facts (How many time zones are there in North America?). Bibliographers call for source citations; students call with research questions; market researchers need statistics. But many other people call strictly for pleasure: to satisfy their curiosity, settle an office bet, or clear up a lifelong mystery (What does *Kemo Sabe* mean?).

The phone lines are often busy; at peak hours, only patient callers get through. Once they do get through, they can rely on the information they get. The staff is not allowed to answer from memory, lore, or educated guesses; every answer must be grounded in fact and verified in print. When they don't know, they tell you. They may refer you to one of the Library's other divisions (such as Business or Science) for help on researching an involved question. Or they may spend days or weeks trying to find the answer themselves. Once they have it, they inscribe it in the margin of a reference book or in their card catalog of hard-to-find facts. (Who came up with the typist's exercise, "Now is the time for all good men to come to the aid of the party"?)

Thus the New York Public Library Telephone Reference Service manages to be what most people would like to be—well versed and reliable. For those of us who fail to meet those criteria, *The Book of Answers* offers more than 1,000 of the Reference Service's most popular, strange, and humorous questions.

The Book of Answers lacks the high seriousness of a dictionary and the exhaustiveness of an encyclopedia. Some of its questions are frequently asked, but some are downright rare. (For a full compendium of frequently sought information, see *The New York Public Library Desk Reference*.) Most of the questions, however, are entertaining, and all are based on questions people actually ask. Are geisha girls prostitutes? What is the world's second-longest river? And for the last time, how long was the Hundred Years' War?

The Book of Answers is structured to reflect the subject areas of the Library and the concerns of its callers. There are the standard academic categories—American History, Science, and Geography. There are the less scholarly arcana that keep Tel Ref librarians busy—Trademarks, Popular Culture, and Crime and Criminals. One section answers questions about ancient and modern celebrities (Who Was Who), another about the Library's hometown (New York City History). Twelve Trick Questions and Popular Delusions explodes a variety of common mistakes. The Library Omnibus offers facts that will fit nowhere else. The Question and Answer Hall of Fame answers the questions people never seem to stop asking.

There are some questions *The Book of Answers* can't answer (What does life mean? When is my wife's birthday?). But it can answer some of the other questions that have stumped you and the Library's millions of callers. When the encyclopedia doesn't have it and the Library's lines are busy, *The Book of Answers* may tell you exactly what you want to know.

—Melinda Corey and George Ochoa

• 1 •

AMERICAN HISTORY

◆◆◆◆◆

Who was the first American-born child of English settlers?
Virginia Dare, born in 1587 to English settlers of the "lost colony" of Roanoke Island. The entire colony disappeared; Dare's death date is unknown.

Did the pilgrims eat turkey at the first Thanksgiving celebration at Plymouth Rock?
At the three-day festivities celebrating survival through the winter, many foods were served, but turkey was not one of them. The menu included: venison, duck, goose, seafood, eels, white bread, corn bread, leeks, watercress and various other greens, wild plums, dried berries, and wine.

Is it true that Manhattan Island was bought from the Indians for $24?
What Peter Minuit gave the Manhattoe tribe was a package of trinkets and cloth valued at 60 guilders—roughly equivalent to $24.

Who founded the city of Chicago?

A black man from Haiti named Jean Baptiste Pointe Du Sable (1745–1818). In 1772, Du Sable founded a settlement called Eschikagou on the north bank of the Chicago River. However, he was not officially recognized as the city's founder until 1968.

Who was the founder of Detroit?

Antoine de la Mothe Cadillac, a French explorer and administrator, founded Fort Pontchartrain du Détroit in 1701. The Cadillac automobile is named for him.

Was Pittsburgh named after someone named Pitt? If so, what did he have to do with Pennsylvania?

Pittsburgh was named for William Pitt—even though Pitt never set foot in Pennsylvania. Pitt's actions as a British war minister during the French and Indian War led to the city's founding. He committed money and troops to the war; he mapped out a strategy that included the capture of Fort Duquesne, located where the Allegheny and Monongahela rivers combine to form the Ohio. After this French fort fell in November 1758, a British one was built—Fort Pitt, or Pittsburgh. The city of Pittsburgh still stands on that spot.

What is the oldest existing hospital in America?

Bellevue, on New York City's East Side, is the oldest general hospital in North America. Plans for the hospital date back to 1736, although at that time the building was meant to be only a "Publick Workhouse and House of Correction" near City Hall (located on the site of present-day City Hall Park). In 1816, a larger space was needed and construction began at Belle Vue Farm, on the hospital's present site.

When were the first African slaves brought to the United States?

In 1619, a Dutch ship brought the first 20 slaves to the English colony of Virginia.

> *How many slaves were freed after the American Civil War?*
> About 4 million.

> *In total, how many Africans were brought to the United States as slaves?*
> Approximately 15 million.

How many Liberty Bells have there been?

Two. The first was cast in England in 1752 for the Pennsylvania State House, which later became Independence Hall. The second was cast in Philadelphia and inscribed, "Proclaim liberty throughout all the land unto all the inhabitants thereof" (Leviticus 25:10). The bell cracked on July 8, 1835, as it tolled the passing of Chief Justice John Marshall.

In the song "Yankee Doodle," why did Yankee Doodle stick a feather in his cap and call it macaroni?

The line refers not to the pasta but to the Macaroni Club, a mid-eighteenth-century English social club of dandyish young men who wanted to bring the influences of the Continent to bear on their home country. Thus the line was originally intended to discredit American revolutionaries.

Did Betsy Ross design the American flag?

No, it was designed by Francis Hopkinson, a naval flag designer, who was never reimbursed for his services by the U.S. government. And there is no record of Betsy Ross's commission to sew the flag.

In the American Revolution, how many men were required for a regiment in the Continental army?

In November 1775, the Continental Congress advised that a regiment have eight companies of 91 officers and men apiece, for a total of 728. The actual size of the regiments varied per state.

How many American casualties were suffered in the American Revolution?

Unofficial studies of field reports indicate that about 4,500 men died in battle and over 6,000 were wounded. Illness also took a large but indeterminate number. At Valley Forge, for example, illness claimed over 3,000 lives.

How many Americans fought for the British in the American Revolution?

Approximately 50,000 Americans were part of the Loyalist military support for the king. Few joined the British army and navy, but thousands served in provincial regiments under Loyalist officers. American Indians—mainly in Canada, on the frontier, and in the South—also fought for Britain.

How much was Benedict Arnold given to be a traitor?

Benedict Arnold (1741–1801) demanded £20,000 from the British but received only £6,315. In exchange, he revealed American battle plans, tried (but failed) to deliver West Point, and crossed over to the British army. Although Arnold was given 13,400 acres of land in Canada after the war, he lived the rest of his life in England.

When was the first U.S. census taken?

In 1790. It included six questions and recorded a population of 3,929,214 persons, of whom 3,172,006 were white and 757,208 were black. The white population was evenly divided between males and females—1,615,434 males, 1,556,572 females. Virginia was the most populous state, with 747,610 inhabitants.

When did the first strike in the United States take place?

In 1776, in New York, when members of the Journeymen Printers Union struck against their local shops.

Where and when was the greatest earthquake in American history?

The largest earthquake in American history was the Great Alaskan Earthquake of 1964. The quake, on

March 28, 1964, had its epicenter near Anchorage and measured a 9.2 on the Richter scale. This is the second highest magnitude ever recorded, behind a 9.5 earthquake in Chile.

How did American currency come to be called dollars and cents?

Dollar was the English spelling of the German *Taler* (a silver coin first issued in 1519). American colonists used the word *dollar* to describe the Spanish peso circulating from South America, and when it came time to devise a system of currency (in 1792), the United States government adopted the dollar as its basic monetary unit. The word *cent* meant one-hundredth of a dollar—following the decimal system of coinage first proposed by Gouverneur Morris (1752–1816). Morris was a New York–born statesman who served as assistant to the superintendent of finance under the Articles of Confederation, from 1781 to 1785.

When did the motto In God We Trust start appearing on U.S. coins?

It has appeared on most American coins since about 1864. During the Civil War, rising popular religious sentiment prompted Secretary of the Treasury Salmon P. Chase to put the country's faith where its money was. Other slogans suggested were God Our Trust and God and Our Country. The motto is not required by law.

How many females have appeared on U.S. currency?

Aside from the female representations of Justice and Liberty, only three women have been so commemorated: Martha Washington, on the face of the 1886 and 1891 $1 silver certificates and on the reverse of the 1896 silver certificate; Pocahontas, on the back of the 1875 $20 bill; and women's suffrage leader Susan B. Anthony, on the 1979 $1 coin.

When was the U.S. Navy established?

An American "Continental Navy" was established by the Second Continental Congress on October 13, 1775. It was disbanded after the War of Independence, in 1784. The first U.S. Navy was not established until April 30, 1798.

How did the elephant and donkey come to be the symbols for the Republican and Democratic parties?

Cartoonist and illustrator Thomas Nast (1840–1902) popularized both symbols but invented only one of them. Democrat Andrew Jackson first used the donkey as a symbol for his party after his opponents in the 1828 presidential election called him a "jackass"; Nast's cartoons later helped to make the symbol famous. Nast himself introduced the Republican elephant in an 1874 cartoon. At first, the elephant was only meant to symbolize the overwhelming strength of "the Republican Vote"; it soon came to stand for the Republican party as a whole.

Has the U.S. Supreme Court ever had more (or fewer) than nine members?

Yes. Originated by the Constitution, the Court has been regulated in size by Congress. The number of justices varied—from six to ten—until 1869, when Congress voted to set the membership at nine.

What was the first chartered railroad in the United States?

The Granite Railway, which began running from Quincy, Massachusetts, to the Neponset River—a distance of three miles—on October 7, 1826. Its principal cargo consisted of blocks of granite for use in building the Bunker Hill Monument in Charlestown. The railway later became part of the New York, New Haven, and Hartford Railroad.

How long did the Pony Express last?

The system of mail delivery by horse-and-rider relays lasted only 18 months, from April 1860 to October 1861. It connected Saint Joseph, Missouri, with Sacramento, California—a distance of 1,800 miles. The completion of the transcontinental telegraph system brought the Pony Express to an end.

Is it true that Robert E. Lee was offered command of both sides in the Civil War?

Yes. Within the span of a few days in April 1861, Lee was offered command of both the Union and Confederate forces. Although he opposed slavery and secession and believed the South could not win, his loyalty to his home state of Virginia led him to accept the Confederate command.

How many people were present at Lincoln's Gettysburg Address?

Approximately 5,000 people appeared at the dedication of the Civil War battlefield cemetery on November 19, 1863.

How many people died at the infamous Andersonville Prison?

More than 13,000 Union prisoners died at Andersonville, the largest Confederate military prison. Most died of neglect. The prison's commandant, Captain Henry Wirz, was the only Civil War soldier executed for war crimes.

When was the Gilded Age?

It was during and just after the administration of President Ulysses S. Grant (1869–1871). So called for its materialism and political corruption, the period was given its name in a satirical novel, *The Gilded Age* (1873), written by Mark Twain with Charles Dudley Warner.

Did a cow really start the great Chicago fire of October 8, 1871?

While the fire did begin in a cow barn behind the cottage of Patrick O'Leary, there is no evidence that a cow was responsible. In fact, a reporter, Michael Ahern, later admitted he created the legend in order to make a better story. The fire lasted 27 hours, killing 250 people and destroying 17,450 buildings.

For how long were there stockyards in Chicago?

For 107 years, beginning in 1864, the mile-square Union Stock Yards stood at Halsted Street and Exchange Avenue. The Swift, Armour, and Wilson companies had plants there. The yards closed on July 31, 1971, and were demolished. Only the Union Stock Yards' gate was preserved; it was named a Chicago landmark on February 24, 1972.

Where did the Chisholm Trail run?

Named for trader Jesse Chisholm, this nineteenth-century cattle route started south of San Antonio, Texas, passed through Oklahoma, and ended at Abilene, Kansas. In 1871—the trail's busiest year—700,000 cattle were driven along the route by 5,000 cowboys.

Where did the Hatfields and McCoys live?

The families lived on opposite sides of a stream called Tug Fork in the Appalachian Mountains. The McCoys resided in Pike County, Kentucky, and the Hatfields in Logan County, West Virginia. How the feud got started is not known, but it got under way in earnest with the killing of a Hatfield in 1882. The fighting went on intermittently into the 1890s and was not completely over until after 1910.

In what town did the gunfight at the O.K. Corral take place, and who was shot?

The famous shootout on October 26, 1881, happened in Tombstone, Arizona Territory, at a photographer's studio just to the east of the O.K. Corral—Camillus Fly's studio. The Earp brothers—Wyatt, Virgil, Morgan—and friend Doc Holliday shot Billy Clanton and neighbors Tom and Frank McLaury. Although there was bad blood between the Earps, the Clantons, and the McLaurys, the Earps shot the three without provocation. The Earps and Holliday were legally cleared of any crime.

What was the Haymarket incident?

It took place on May 4, 1886, at Chicago's Haymarket Square during a peaceful rally to protest the killing three days earlier of six workers striking for the eight-hour day. Two hundred policemen were sent in to break up the rally. Before they could, a dynamite bomb of unknown origin exploded, killing 8 policemen and wounding 65 others, and also killing an undetermined number of civilians. Seven labor leaders were held responsible and condemned to death. Two had their sentences commuted to life; four were hanged; one killed himself.

When was the U.S. government given the right to tax its citizens?

It happened in 1913 by way of the 16th Amendment to the Constitution:

The Congress shall have power to lay and collect taxes, from whatever source derived, without apportionment among the several States, and without regard to any census or enumeration.

What was the first minimum wage?

When it was instituted in 1938, the minimum wage was 25 cents per hour.

When did "The Star-Spangled Banner" become the national anthem?

The four-stanza song was adopted as the national anthem by the U.S. Congress in 1931. Francis Scott Key wrote the lyrics in 1814, taking the melody from an eighteenth-century drinking song called "To Anacreon in Heaven" by British composer John Stafford Smith. (Anacreon was a Greek lyric poet [563–478 B.C.] associated with love and wine.)

Who wrote the Pledge of Allegiance?

It was written by Francis Bellamy, editor of the children's magazine *The Youth's Companion,* for its September 8, 1892, issue, to commemorate Columbus Day. It originally read: "I pledge allegiance to my Flag and the Republic for which it stands—one nation indivisible—with liberty and justice for all." The verse became a popular Columbus Day tradition and, later, a daily school recitation. In 1923, the U.S. Flag Association replaced "my flag" with "the flag of the United States of America," and in 1954, Congress added "under God."

Did the United States have warning of the attack on Pearl Harbor?

Ten hours before the surprise attack on December 7, 1941, Americans intercepted a 14-part Japanese message. They deciphered it at 4:37 A.M., Washington time, just hours before the attack, but the message remained in the code room; not until three hours later was it delivered to President Roosevelt. By 11:00 A.M., the U.S. chief of naval operations and the army chief of staff received the deciphered message, which was then transmitted to all areas of the Pacific except Hawaii, where the receiver was not working. The message did not reach Pearl Harbor until nearly three hours after the attack, which took 3,000 lives.

Who wrote the U.S. Supreme Court decision outlawing school segregation?

Brown v. Board of Education of Topeka, Kansas, was written by U.S. Supreme Court Chief Justice Earl Warren (1891–1974). Delivered on May 17, 1954, it was one of the first of several major decisions of the Warren Court, which lasted from 1953 to 1969.

When did the last Americans leave Vietnam? When did the government of South Vietnam surrender?

The last Americans—about 1,000—were evacuated from Saigon on April 29, 1975. The Saigon government surrendered a few hours later.

How many Americans died in the Vietnam War?

According to the U.S. Department of Defense, 58,135 Americans were killed and 153,303 wounded. It is estimated that 1.3 million Vietnamese lost their lives.

During Gerald R. Ford's presidency, what did the *WIN* in the WIN buttons stand for?
Whip Inflation Now.

How long were the 52 American hostages held in Teheran, Iran?
They were held for 444 days, from November 4, 1979, to January 20, 1981, the day Ronald Reagan was inaugurated president.

How much has the U.S. national debt increased over the nation's history?
In 1800, the national debt was $83 million. In 1988, it was $2.6 trillion.

◆ 2 ◆

AMERICAN STATISTICS

◆◆◆◆◆

Is Chicago the windiest city in the United States?
Far from it. With an average wind speed of 10.4 miles per hour, Chicago ranks 16th in the list of windy American cities. Here are the top five, with average wind speeds (in miles per hour):

1. *Great Falls, Montana.* 13.1
2. *Oklahoma City, Oklahoma.* 13
3. *Boston, Massachusetts.* 12.9
4. *Cheyenne, Wyoming.* 12.8
5. *Wichita, Kansas.* 12.7

What do Americans fear most?
A poll of 3,000 Americans yielded the following top five fears:

1. *Speaking before a group.* 41 percent
2. *Heights.* 32 percent

3. *Insects and bugs.* 22 percent
4. *Financial problems.* 22 percent
5. *Deep water.* 22 percent

What are the three most popular natural attractions in the United States?

They rank as follows:

1. *The Grand Canyon* (Arizona)
2. *Yellowstone National Park* (Wyoming)
3. *Niagara Falls* (New York)

Which U.S. states have the greatest number of hazardous waste sites?

In descending order, the top five are:

1. *New Jersey.* 96
2. *New York.* 63
3. *Pennsylvania.* 61
4. *Michigan.* 58
5. *California.* 48

Which states or territories had the highest presidential voter turnout in 1988? Which had the lowest?

The three states or territories with the highest voter turnout in the 1988 presidential election, in descending order, were:

1. *Minnesota.* 66.3 percent
2. *Montana.* 62.41 percent
3. *Maine.* 62.15 percent

The three states or territories with the lowest turnout, in ascending order, were:

1. *Georgia.* 38.79 percent
2. *South Carolina.* 38.91 percent
3. *District of Columbia.* 39.44 percent

Which age group in the United States has the highest voter turnout?

According to 1980 census findings, citizens in the 55-to-64 age group had a turnout of 71.3 percent. Close behind were those in the 65-to-74 age group, with 69.3 percent. Those 18 and 19 brought up the rear with a 34.2 percent showing.

What are the three tallest buildings in the United States?

Sears Tower. 1,454 feet, 110 stories (Chicago)
World Trade Center. 1,350 feet, 110 stories (New York)
Empire State Building. 1,250 feet, 102 stories (New York)

Which U.S. state has the highest per-capita personal income? The lowest?

Connecticut was number one in 1987 with $20,980. At the bottom was Mississippi with $10,204. The average per-capita personal income in the United States as a whole was $15,340.

What is the largest U.S. city in area?

It is not New York, Chicago, or Los Angeles. It is Juneau, Alaska, which covers 3,108 square miles. Los Angeles, in contrast, covers only 458.2 square miles.

How much water does the average American use every day?

For drinking, washing, etc., an average American uses 168 gallons per day. The average American residence uses 107,000 gallons per year.

How much of America drinks fluoridated water?

As of 1990, 53 percent of Americans drink fluoridated water. Of these, 121 million drink artificially fluoridated water; 9 million drink water from naturally fluoridated sources.

Has New York always been the nation's most populous city?

Yes—at least since 1800. At that time, Philadelphia and Baltimore were the second- and third-largest cities. Census estimates for 1986 placed Los Angeles and Chicago, respectively, in those ranks.

What is the most popular month for births in the United States?

According to 1980 figures, August registered 9.2 percent of the year's births. The second most popular month was October, with 9 percent of the year's births.

How does the marriage rate in the United States in recent years compare to that in 1900? The divorce rate?

Recent marriage rates have been fairly similar to what they were at the turn of the century. In 1900, the marriage rate was 9.3 per 1,000; in 1988, it was 9.7. The divorce rate, however, has changed drastically. In 1900, it was 0.7 per 1,000; in 1988, it was 4.8.

Do American women still earn less money than American men?

Yes. In 1988, the median weekly earnings of full-time female workers in all occupations were 70.2 percent of male workers' earnings.

In an average year, how many Americans are audited?

In 1980, the Internal Revenue Service audited 1,528,927 returns, 1.9 percent of all returns submitted. The IRS claimed in 1980 it spends $4.40 for every $1,000 it collects from taxpayers.

How many people in America receive food stamps?

Census estimates for 1986 revealed that 6,779,000 of a total 88,458,000 households, or 7.66 percent, received food stamps during the year.

Which federal agency employs the most people? The fewest?

As of May 1988, the Department of Defense employed the most, with 1,066,805 civilian employees. The

Copyright Royalty Tribunal employed the fewest, with seven.

On an average day, how much mail is handled by the U.S. Post Office?

According to the Report of the Postmaster General, 106,311,062,000 pieces of mail traveled through the system in 1980. On a given day, therefore, approximately 291,263,000 items passed through the country's post offices. What's more, this prodigious amount of mail traveled through many fewer post offices than at the turn of the century. In 1900, there were 76,688 post offices; in 1980, there were 30,326.

How many members of the U.S. military are on active duty?

As of 1988, 764,247 persons were on active duty.

How far can a U.S. Army Pershing missile travel?

The 34.5-foot, 10,000-pound surface-to-surface missile has a range of approximately 400 miles.

How does the average American travel to work and how long does it take?

According to 1980 figures, the average worker's one-way trip covered 9.2 miles and took 20.4 minutes. By far the favorite mode of transportation for workers was the private vehicle (car, motorcycle, or truck), accounting for 84.3 percent. Those who took public transportation comprised 6.3 percent, and 5.5 percent walked. The remainder used other means or worked at home.

How many dogs and cats are there in the United States?

In 1988, the United States was home to 49.4 million dogs and 57.8 million cats. The percentage of American households owning dogs was 37.2; the percentage owning cats was 30.

Which two points in the contiguous United States are farthest apart?

Cape Flattery, Washington, and a point on the Florida coast south of Miami. They are 2,835 miles apart.

What is the geographic center of the United States?

The center of the 48 contiguous states is in Smith County, Kansas, near the town of Lebanon. The center of the 50 states is in Butte County, South Dakota, west of the town of Castle Rock.

What is the northernmost point of the United States?

Point Barrow, a city in Alaska with a 1980 population of 2,207, mostly Eskimo. It was the site of the 1935 air crash that killed Will Rogers.

How long are the two U.S. borders?

The length of the Canadian border is 3,987 miles. The length of the Mexican border is 1,933 miles.

What are the highest and lowest elevations in the United States?

The highest elevation is Mount McKinley, Alaska, at 20,320 feet. The lowest is Death Valley, California, at 282 feet below sea level. The average elevation of the United States is 2,500 feet.

How many national forests have been established in the United States?

Started in 1891 by President Theodore Roosevelt, the national system of forest reserves now consists of 154 forests administered by the Department of Agriculture's Forest Service. The total area of the reserves is over 343,000 square miles.

What is the most despised household task?

According to a Gallup poll, washing the dishes far outweighs its closest competitors, cleaning the bathroom and ironing. Seventeen percent of those questioned listed doing the dishes first; only 8.8 percent named cleaning the bathroom and 8.5 percent named ironing, with 9.8 percent saying they didn't know what they didn't like.

• 3 •

THE ANIMAL WORLD

••••••

How fast can a turkey run?

The wild turkey, the breed indigenous to the United States, weighs 50 to 60 pounds, has strong legs, and can run from 15 to 20 miles per hour when scared.

How far can a kangaroo jump?

Large kangaroos cover more than 30 feet with each jump. One large kangaroo was measured as clearing a pile of timber 10.5 feet high and 27 feet long.

Do hens sit on eggs?

After a fashion. They squat on the eggs, supporting most of their weight with their feet. Their nests also provide a protective cushion for the eggs.

Is a dog year really seven human years?

No, it is actually five to six years. The average life expectancy of a dog is 12 to 14 years. However, most dogs mature sexually within six to nine months so in that sense there is no strict correspondence to human years.

Is the phrase *dog days* related to dogs?

It dates back to Roman times, when it was believed that Sirius, the Dog Star, added its heat to that of the sun from July 3 to August 11, creating exceptionally high temperatures. The Romans called the period *dies caniculares*, or "days of the dog."

Which dogs bite the most?

A 27-year New York City study found that the following five breeds—in order of biting averages—are the worst offenders:

1. German police dog
2. Chow
3. Poodle
4. Italian bulldog
5. Fox terrier

Which dogs bite the least?

1. Golden retriever
2. Labrador retriever
3. Shetland sheepdog
4. Old English sheepdog
5. Welsh terrier

How do you tell the sex of a cat?

Raise its tail. If you see what looks like a colon (the punctuation mark), you're probably looking at a male. If you see an upside-down semicolon, it's a female.

How do you tell the age of a fish?

The scales provide the best clue. Scaleless when born, fish grow scales under their outer layer of skin to provide waterproofing. As they age, most species add growth rings—that is, increase the size of their scales to cover their larger bodies. With a very old fish, however, there are fewer additions, making it difficult to pinpoint its age. This method also does not work for fish without scales, such as catfish.

How old is the species of fish known as the *coelacanth*?

This ancient creature existed 350 million years ago. Scientists had believed that the fish became extinct 60 million years ago, until a living specimen was caught in the Indian Ocean off southern Africa in 1938.

What is the world's largest rodent?

The *capybara*, also known as the carpincho or water hog, native to South America. In length, it runs from 3 feet, 3 inches to 4 feet, 6 inches, and it weighs up to 174 pounds. The only other rodent of similar size is the Canadian beaver, the largest specimen of which is recorded at 87 pounds.

What was the biggest pig in recorded history?
It was Big Boy of Black Mountain, North Carolina, weighing 1,904 pounds in 1939.

Why do bulls charge when they "see red"?
Bulls do not charge because a cape is red. They charge because of the *movement* of the cape. It does not have to be red or any other bright color.

Do animals see color?
Apes and some monkeys perceive the full spectrum of color, as may some fish and birds. But most mammals view color only as shades of gray.

How slow is a crab?
A crab of the species *Neptunus pelagines* took 29 years to walk 101.5 miles underwater from the Red Sea to the Mediterranean—an average speed of 3.5 miles per year.

What is the largest cockroach on record?
At 3.81 inches in length, this one could hardly check into a Roach Motel, much less check out.

Does a centipede really have 100 legs? Does a millipede have 1,000?
No, the number of legs varies. The greatest number reported on a centipede is 171 to 177 pairs of legs; on a millipede, 375.

Do female black widow spiders kill and eat their mates after sex?
Sometimes. What makes them decide to do so is uncertain.

What are the formal names for groups of bears, cats, crows, gnats, kangaroos, peacocks, and swine?

A sleuth or sloth of bears
A clutter or chowder of cats
A murder of crows
A cloud or horde of gnats
A troop of kangaroos
A muster or ostentation of peacocks
A sounder of swine

Which mammal has the longest life span?
There are rare instances of elephants living 70 years and killer whales 90, but humans, with their outside limit of about 120 years, have the longest overall life span.

What is the shortest known gestation period of any mammal? What is the longest?
The American opossum, a marsupial, bears its young 12 to 13 days after conception. The Asiatic elephant takes 608 days, or just over 20 months.

What makes cats purr?
In addition to being a sign of contentment, it is a signal, a homing call that cats learn early. At first, they

feel only the vibrations of a purr when their mother cat uses it to bring them to feed. Later, cats learn to use it to indicate fear and distress as well as pleasure.

How fast can birds fly?

Spine-tailed swifts have been clocked at speeds of up to 220 miles per hour. Peregrine falcons have reached 217 miles per hour; racing pigeons, 100; migrating ducks, 60; and small birds, 30.

Why do birds sing?

In most species of songbirds, only male birds sing, and for only two reasons: to protect territory and to attract a mate.

What good do termites do?

More efficiently than any other wood-eating creature, termites clear fallen timber and stumps from forests. They can clear vast quantities of wood that otherwise would be left to rot.

What is the difference between a crocodile and an alligator?

The alligator is a subspecies of the crocodile, part of the family Crocodylidae. The alligator's snout is rounded; the crocodile's comes to a point. Both prefer shallow, swampy water, but the crocodile is generally more aggressive than the alligator. Incidentally, a crocodile, not an alligator, appears on the Izod Lacoste polo shirt.

How fast do piranhas eat?

A school of these 8- to 12-inch fish, which inhabit the freshwater rivers of South America, has been observed gnawing a 400-pound hog to the bone in minutes. Initially attracted by the smell of blood, piranhas begin gnawing as soon as they reach their prey. With their spring-trap jaws, they remove any animal's flesh most efficiently.

When did the dodo become extinct?

Not until 1681, and mainly because humans and animals ate the remaining eggs. The dodo, first found on the island of Mauritius in the Indian Ocean, was the size of a very large turkey. It was slow and defenseless, save for its hooked beak. To complicate matters, it did not reproduce well, as the female laid only one egg each year. The death knell came in the 1600s, however, when Dutch colonists on Mauritius found the eggs palatable. Other animals also found them edible, and soon the dodo was gone.

How large a tree can a beaver cut down?

Beavers prefer slender poplar trees for food, but will cut down trees as large as 18 inches in diameter, including hardwoods such as beech, cherry, and oak.

What kind of fish is a sardine?

The term applies to several species of the herring family, including the common herring of the North Atlantic, the European pilchard, and members of the genus *Sardinops* found in the Pacific and Indian oceans.

What is the purpose of a skunk's scent?

The skunk uses his special body oil to defeat enemies that are larger, faster, and stronger than he is. The oil burns an attacker's eyes, nose, and mouth, causing temporary blindness and vomiting. This fluid accumulates in the skunk's scent glands, which contain enough for six shots from distances of 8 to 10 feet.

What is the largest living animal?

The largest animal ever seen alive was a 113.5-foot, 170-ton female blue whale. The whale is able to reach such large size because water helps support its weight.

What does the Chihuahua dog have to do with the Mexican state of Chihuahua?

The smallest recognized breed of dog was first noted in Chihuahua in northern Mexico in the mid-nineteenth century. The dog is believed to be descended from the Techichi, a small mute dog kept by the Toltec people of Mexico since the ninth century A.D.

How did the dachshund get its name?

The modern name for one of the oldest dog breeds in history (dating back to ancient Egypt) arose from one of its earliest uses—hunting badgers. In German, *Dachs* means "badger," *Hund* is "hound." Centuries ago, badger hunting was a popular sport.

Can any creatures besides humans get a sunburn?
Only pigs have humans' intolerance of the sun.

Do birds sing only in trees?
No—some species sing on the ground. Shorebirds such as turnstones sing from mounds called hummocks. Some species of American field sparrows, such as the savanna sparrow of the eastern United States, sing from the ground, as does the wood thrush.

What is a nutria?
Ratlike in appearance and beaverlike in size, this animal is often referred to as the beaver rat. Nutrias are valuable for many purposes; their pelts are now chiefly used in the making of hats. Their ratlike tails are too thin to be used.

Do Siamese fighting fish fight?
The males do. They nip each other's fins and show off their extended gill covers and intensified colors. Their battles are exciting enough that the Thai have domesticated the fish for use in contests.

Do fish sleep?
Most fish do not. They are constantly in motion, though the motion is marked by periods of reduced activity. There are, however, a few exceptions: Some fish in coral reefs do sleep by leaning on rocks or standing on their tails.

Do different species have different colors of blood?
Yes. The blood of mammals is red, the blood of insects is yellow, and the blood of lobsters is blue.

What was the first animal to be listed as an endangered species in the United States?
The peregrine falcon was listed as endangered in the late 1970s. It still remains on the list.

When does a pig become a hog?
In the United States, all swine weighing under 180 pounds are pigs; those over that weight are hogs. In Britain, there is no difference: The term *pig* refers to all domestic swine.

What kind of cat is a polecat?
It is not a cat at all. Polecat is the common name for various weasellike animals of the family Mustelidae, which also includes weasels, minks, and otters. Varieties of this creature include: the European polecat; the mashed, or steppe, polecat of Asia; the marbled polecat of Eurasia; and the zorilla, or African polecat. In the United States, skunks are often referred to as polecats.

How large do tapeworms get?
They range in size from about 0.04 inch to more than 50 feet in length.

Do tarantulas spin webs?
It depends. The Italian species of wolf spider first given the name *tarantula* (from the town of Taranto) catches

its prey by pursuit. In the American Southwest, tarantulas live in burrows; they eat anything from insects to toads and mice. However, certain South American tarantulas do build large webs; their diet includes small birds.

What exactly is a Tasmanian devil?

It is a marsupial, 20 to 31 inches long, with black-brown hair, a bushy tail, and a bearlike face. It lives in rocky parts of Tasmania, an island south of Australia, and eats small animals and carrion. It is called a devil because of its nasty expression, husky snarl, and bad temper.

What is the most common species of domesticated bird?

It is the chicken. There are thought to be 3.5 billion chickens in the world, nearly one for every human.

How fast can a snake move?

The black mamba of southern Africa has been said to move 25 to 30 miles per hour while chasing a man on horseback.

How far can a frog jump?

The world record is 33 feet 5.5 inches over the course of three consecutive leaps, achieved in May 1977 by a South African sharp-nosed frog called Santjie.

What is the largest shark attack ever recorded?

On November 28, 1942, hundreds of British seamen and Italian prisoners of war were killed by sharks when a German U-boat sank the steamer *Nova Scotia* off the coast of South Africa. Nine hundred men were on the ship when it sank; 192 were left when a rescue ship arrived.

How do archer fish "shoot" their victims?

Archer fish, members of the five species of the family Toxotidae, shoot arcs of water droplets at insects sitting on vegetation near lakes and streams, thereby, knocking them into the water where they become easy prey.

Where in a whale can you find ambergris?

The valuable substance is found in the stomach of a sperm whale. In the East, the soft, black ambergris is dried and used as a spice; in the West, it is used as a perfume fixative.

What is the most unlikely mating between dogs on record?

In 1972, in South Wales, a male dachshund is said to have crept up on a sleeping female Great Dane. The union produced 13 "Great Dachshunds," with short legs, large heads, and raised ears.

◆ 4 ◆

CRIME AND CRIMINALS

◆◆◆◆◆

Where did gangster Al Capone get the scar on his cheek?

Al ("Scarface") Capone claimed he received the scar while fighting with the Lost Battalion in France during World War I. Actually, he was knifed in Brooklyn while working as a bouncer in a saloon—in a fight over a woman. Capone never served in World War I.

How long did the Saint Valentine's Day Massacre last?

Eight minutes. Several members of the George ("Bugs") Moran gang were killed that day, February 14, 1929, along with a man in the garage who looked like Moran. Moran himself escaped the massacre to die a natural death of lung cancer on February 25, 1957.

How long has the FBI been in operation?

An agency called the Bureau of Investigation was instituted in 1908 by President Theodore Roosevelt, who believed that the federal government should have an arm to enforce federal law. It was renamed the Federal Bureau of Investigation in 1935. Twenty-nine-year-old J. Edgar Hoover became its first acting director in 1924.

When was the FBI's Ten Most Wanted List started?

In 1950. In 1970, the FBI unofficially increased the number to 16.

What does the word *Mafia* mean? What does the word *Cosa Nostra* mean?

In Italian, *Mafia* means "beauty, excellence, bravery"; *Cosa Nostra* means "our thing."

What is the difference between the Black Hand and the Mafia?

The Black Hand was the name for groups of extortionists who preyed upon Italian immigrants in the United States from about 1890 to 1920. It was active in cities such as Chicago, Kansas City, New Orleans, and New York. The Mafia, an older and more complex criminal organization, originated in Sicily in the nineteenth and early twentieth centuries. In some phases of its history, it provided a system of justice in a Sicily ruled by despotic regimes.

What was the White Hand Society?

A community group sponsored by Italian-American business leaders, it was organized in 1907 to oppose the work of the Black Hand. It developed its own police force but sustained itself for only five years.

Who are the five Mafia families of New York City?

The Bonanno, Colombo, Gambino, Genovese, and Lucchese families.

When did the murders of Jack the Ripper occur?

The throat-slashings of six prostitutes in London's East End occurred between August and early November 1888. The identity of Jack the Ripper was never verified.

Who was known as the .44-Caliber Killer?

It was "Son of Sam" killer David Richard Berkowitz (b. 1953), who from July 1976 to August 1977 killed six people and wounded seven others with a .44-caliber gun.

Who was the last person to be branded as punishment for a crime?

In 1844, Jonathan Walker had the initials SS branded into the palm of his right hand. He had been convicted of slave stealing—helping slaves escape to the Bahamas. Branding had been used officially as punishment in America since the seventeenth century.

When did the practice of lynching begin?

While hanging may have occurred earlier in U.S. history, the practice of lynching was probably started by Colonel William Lynch of Virginia in the 1780s. Lynch organized a vigilante band aimed at ridding Pittsylvania County of its bad element. An 1836 editorial by Edgar Allan Poe discusses Lynch's career.

What is an *air dance*?

It is an execution by hanging. Other slang terms for hanging: *air jig, air polka,* and *air rumba.*

What is a *black act*?

It is slang for picking a lock in the dark.

What is a *Chicago overcoat*?

A 1920s underworld term for a coffin.

What is *Chicago amnesia*?

The phrase, coined by 1920s gang leader Dion O'Banion, referred to the convenient forgetfulness of eyewitnesses testifying about gang lawbreakers. The phrase implied that gang members had persuaded the witnesses to forget whatever they had seen.

What causes a death rattle?

A death rattle, the sound a person often makes before dying, is caused by air being forced through food or mucus lodged in the throat.

What is a *last laugh*?

A bullet shot through a victim's heart sometimes precipitates a final laugh before death.

What is a *meat-eater*?

It is slang for a policeman or politician who accepts or extorts graft.

Who are the *state chemists* and *state electricians*?

State chemists are the executioners who kill condemned prisoners by lethal injection. State electricians perform executions by means of the electric chair.

What is the largest bank robbery on record?

On April 22, 1981, in Tucson, Arizona, four gunmen robbed the First National Bank of Arizona of $3.3 million. Wearing Halloween masks and stocking hoods, the gunmen cleaned out a vault containing cash receipts from 27 other First National branches in Tucson.

How did the red-light district get its name?

The red light came from an actual lamp—the red oil-lamp that hung on the last car of a railroad train. These lamps were carried by railroad men to and from trains, and in some cases they were hung outside the brothels the men frequented between shifts.

How long were chain gangs used in America?

Borrowing from eighteenth-century English penal procedures, southern states began using chain gangs before the Civil War and continued the practice for nearly a hundred years. Georgia became the last state to outlaw this method of punishment in the late 1940s. The decline of chain gangs was due as much to automation as to public protest: New machinery used to build roads did not require as many workers.

Why did kidnapped heiress Patty Hearst take the name Tania?

The woman taken from her Berkeley, California, home on February 5, 1974, by the Symbionese Liberation Army adopted the name Tania in honor of Latin American revolutionary Che Guevara's mistress, Tania Guitterez Baer.

What's the origin of the word *hijack*?

During Prohibition, the taking of trucks full of illegal liquor became commonplace. When it happened, a gunman would say, "High, Jack," to indicate how the driver should raise his hands.

Was public kissing ever a crime in the United States?

Yes, and it still is in some places. In 1656 in Boston, a Captain Kimble was placed in the stocks for kissing his wife in public on the Sabbath. To this day, it is illegal in Indiana for a mustached man to "habitually kiss human beings." In Cedar Rapids, Iowa, it is still a crime to kiss a stranger.

When were the Rosenbergs executed?

Julius and Ethel Rosenberg were executed on June 19, 1953, at Sing Sing prison in Ossining, New York. Julius Rosenberg, thirty-five, was executed at 8:04 P.M. His wife, Ethel, thirty-seven, was executed at 8:11 P.M.

When was Lee Harvey Oswald shot?

At about 11:20 A.M. (CST), on November 24, 1963, the twenty-four-year-old Oswald was shot by Dallas nightclub operator Jack Ruby (formerly Rubenstein) as Oswald was being transferred from jail to an armored truck. He was killed by one shot of a .38-caliber snub-nosed revolver.

What was James Earl Ray's sentence for killing Martin Luther King, Jr.?

On March 12, 1969, he was sentenced to 99 years in prison.

Which criminal mastermind was nicknamed Mr. Big?

Arnold Rothstein (1882–1928), who financed the criminal operations of Lucky Luciano, Legs Diamond, and others. Also known as the Brain, the Fixer, and the Man Uptown, Rothstein was said to have played a role in fixing the 1919 World Series.

Who was the original Bluebeard?

He was a wife murderer in Charles Perrault's 1679 novel *Conte du Temps*. The nickname has since been applied to many real-life killers of women. The most famous was Frenchman Henri Désiré Landru (1869–1922), who over a period of five years killed 10 women after proposing marriage to them.

Who was known as the Man Who Shot Dillinger?

FBI agent Melvin Purvis. Purvis never actually fired at Dillinger in the 1934 shootout that ended in the death of "public enemy number one." But Purvis directed the trap and pointed Dillinger out to other agents and police.

How many parolees commit crimes while on parole?

A 1979 New York study revealed that only 3.4 percent of state parolees were returned to prison for committing new crimes; 8.5 percent were returned for parole violations. Thirty percent of ex-prisoners, however, were sent back to prison within five years of their release.

When did Kim Philby become a Soviet spy?

He was recruited by the Russians in the early 1930s. He entered the British Secret Service in 1939 and remained a double agent until 1962, when he escaped to the Soviet Union. His orders, he said, were to penetrate British Intelligence and "it did not matter how long I took to do the job."

What was his real name?
Harold Adrian Russell Philby. He was nicknamed "Kim" after Rudyard Kipling's Indian boy-hero.

What do the following slang terms mean to spies?

Black-Bag Job. An agent's work, from bribery to breaking and entering.

Demote Maximally. To purge an organization by killing.

The Firm. The British Secret Service.

The Company. The CIA.

Measles. A murder handled so deftly that death appears to be accidental or from natural causes.

Legend. An agent's fake biography, used as a cover.

Ladies. Female spies who seek to compromise members of the opposition.

Soap. Specially treated sodium pentothol, or truth serum.

What is MI5? MI6?

MI5 is Britain's counterintelligence service, which operates mainly at home. MI6 is Britain's Secret Service, which operates mainly overseas. The official titles are DI5 and DI6, but the "M" titles—for Military Intelligence, Departments 5 and 6—are what everyone uses.

How did detectives come to be known as private eyes?

The name is derived from the logo for Pinkerton's National Detective Agency—an eye with the slogan, "We Never Sleep." As the fame of the agency (founded in 1850) spread, criminals talked about their fear of "private eyes," as opposed to the public eyes of the police.

Were Sacco and Vanzetti ever pardoned?

Yes—but not until long after their deaths. On July 14, 1921, Nicola Sacco and Bartolomeo Vanzetti, two avowed anarchists, were convicted of robbing a shoe factory and murdering a paymaster and guard in South Braintree, Massachusetts. Their trial was marred by possible perjury, suppression of evidence, and the bias of the judge against foreign-born anarchists. The two defendants were executed on August 23, 1927. Their names were cleared 50 years later in a special proclamation by Massachusetts governor Michael Dukakis.

How did inexpensive handguns come to be called Saturday Night Specials?

Detroit lawmen coined the term in the late 1950s and early 1960s when they realized that Saturday night holdups were committed with handguns purchased in quick one-hour trips to Toledo, Ohio. There, guns could be bought at filling stations and flower shops for $5 or $10, without time restrictions.

What was the decision at the Scopes trial?

John T. Scopes was a young biology teacher in Dayton, Tennessee, who broke a state law forbidding the teaching of evolution. His 11-day trial in 1925 ended with his conviction and a fine of $100. Authorities later reversed the decision on a legal technicality. Prosecuting attorney William Jennings Bryan died five days after the trial ended, following a huge meal.

What became of Leopold and Loeb?

The two young men from Chicago—who, fired with the idea of committing the "perfect murder," killed fourteen-year-old Bobbie Franks in May 1924—were sentenced on September 10 to life imprisonment for murder and 99 years for kidnapping. Richard ("Dickie") Loeb was slashed to death in a brawl in January 1936 in Northern Illinois Penitentiary near Joliet. Nathan ("Babe") Leopold was paroled in March 1958. Claiming he wanted "a chance to find redemption for myself and to help others," he moved to Puerto Rico to work as a hospital technician. He died on August 30, 1971.

Who shoplifts more often—men or women?

For this crime, women outnumber men by four or five to one.

Was Ma Barker ever arrested?

No. Although Mrs. Barker (the former Arizona Donnie Clark) saw three of her four sons serve in Alcatraz, Kansas State Penitentiary at Lansing, and Leavenworth, she stayed behind the scenes of the crimes. She and her son Freddie were killed on January 16, 1935, in a 45-minute gunfight with FBI agents. Her other sons were Arthur ("Doc"), Herman, and Lloyd.

Who made more money from their jobs—John Dillinger or Bonnie and Clyde?

By far, it was Dillinger, whose most successful robbery, in Greencastle, Indiana, yielded $74,000. Bonnie Parker and Clyde Barrow stole from gas stations, lunch counters, and small banks; their top job brought only $1,500.

What were the real names of Butch Cassidy and the Sundance Kid?

Cassidy, the leader of the Hole-in-the-Wall Gang, was born Robert Leroy Parker in Circleville, Utah, on April 1, 1866. He was one of 10 children. The Sundance Kid was born Harry Longbaugh in 1870 in Phoenixville, Pennsylvania.

How did Legs Diamond get his nickname?

Philadelphia-born John T. Noland (1896–1931) earned it early in his career. As a teenager, he joined a gang called the Hudson Dusters, which stole packages from the backs of trucks. For his ability to dodge police in his efforts, he was nicknamed Legs. Diamond was one of his chosen surnames.

How many prisoners in the United States are on death row?

According to the U.S. Bureau of Justice Statistics, the year 1987 saw 1,781 prisoners on death row. Between 1930 and 1980, 3,862 persons were executed in the United States.

• 5 •

THE ENGLISH
LANGUAGE

◆◆◆◆◆

What is the oldest letter in the alphabet? The most recent?

The oldest is *o*—first used by Egyptians in about 3000 B.C. The newest letters are *j* and *v*. The consonant *j* was not distinguished from the vowel *i* until the 1600s, and not until the Renaissance was the consonant *v* distinguished from the vowel *u*.

What are the five most frequently used letters of the alphabet?

In order of frequency of use, they are: *e, t, o, a,* and *n*.

Which letters are least frequently used?
They are: *k, j, x, z,* and *q*.

What does *O.K.* stand for?

Despite many alternative claims, the first appearance in print links the term *O.K.* to a political organization that supported the reelection of President Martin Van Buren. The New York *New Era* of March 23, 1840, carried an article on the Democratic O.K. Club, the initials standing for Old Kinderhook, a Van Buren epithet derived from his birthplace, Kinderhook, in southeastern New York State. During the election campaign, the letters *O.K.* became a favorite, if mysterious, rallying cry.

Where did the word *nice* come from?

It derives from the Latin *nescius*, or "ignorant," which comes from *nescire*, or "not to know." In the fourteenth and fifteenth centuries, the phrase *a nice person* connoted foolishness rather than agreeableness. Over the years, however, *nice* has gained its more favorable, if bland, connotation.

What does *to be hoist by one's own petard* mean?

The word *petard* refers to a type of bomb or mine once used to break down walls and gates. *To be hoist* is to be blown up. Therefore, *to be hoist by one's own petard* is to be, literally or figuratively, blown up by one's own bomb.

What are the genesis and meaning of the phrase *three sheets to the wind*?

The phrase, which has come to refer to a completely inebriated person, derives from sailing—but not from the sails, as one might think. In the early 1800s, chains were used to regulate the angle of the sails, and these were called sheets. When the sheets were loose, the boat would become unstable and "tipsy," thereby resembling a drunk person.

What do you call the covering on the end of a shoelace?

An aglet.

> *The metal hoop that supports a lampshade?*
> A harp.

> *The indentation at the bottom of a wine bottle?*
> A kick or a punt.

What is the name of the instrument shoe salespeople use to measure feet?

The metal measurer is called the Brannock device.

What is the origin of the phrase 23-Skiddoo?

It was coined by New York's Finest along Twenty-third Street in the years before World War I. At the corner of Twenty-third Street and Broadway—traditionally the windiest corner of the city—men used to stand outside the famous Flatiron Building for free looks at ladies' well-turned ankles. The police dutifully moved the audience along, thus giving rise to the phrase.

Did the word *shyster* come from Shakespeare's Shylock?

No, it came from a Mr. Scheuster, an unscrupulous American criminal lawyer in the 1840s.

Did the use of *lush* for a drunkard originate with someone named Lush?

Yes—Dr. Thomas Lushington (1590–1661), an English chaplain who liked his liquor. The City of Lushington, a London drinking club, may have borrowed its name from him. In the nineteenth century, the City of Lushington in turn became the source of the word *lush*—originally a slang term for beer and eventually another word for drunkard.

What is a papal bull?

It is not an animal, but an official edict or decree from a pope. The term comes from the Latin *bulla* (a knob or seal), and it originally referred to the seal that was placed on the pope's official documents.

How did the phrase *bringing home the bacon* originate?

There are several theories. One is that the phrase refers to greased-pig contests once held at county fairs, where the winner kept the pig and thus *brought home the bacon*. Another theory revolves around the town of Dunmon, England. There, in A.D. 1111, a noblewoman decreed that any person who knelt at the church door and swore that "for 12 months and a day he has never had a household brawl or wished himself unmarried" could claim a side of bacon. Thus, a man who *brought home the bacon* from Dunmon was, at least according to his own oath, enjoying a good marriage. Over the five centuries in which records for this event were kept, only eight people won the prize. Yet another possibility is that the phrase stems from the eighteenth-century use of *bacon* as a slang term for the rewards brought home by a criminal.

What is the origin of the term *baker's dozen?*

The term probably dates back to fifteenth-century England, where strict laws were passed to prohibit bakers from underweighing their bread. Since weights could not be precise, bakers adopted the practice of giving 13 loaves on every order of 12. However, another theory has to do with the common folk phrase *devil's dozen*, meaning 13. Bakers of the Middle Ages were in such bad repute that the words *baker* and *devil* were synonymous. Thus a devil's dozen could also be called a baker's dozen.

Why is the head groomsman at a wedding called the best man? Why isn't there a best woman?

The phrase *best man* is of Scottish origin and recalls the days when a bridegroom simply kidnapped the woman he wanted as his bride. To help him in that task, the groom enlisted a cadre of friends. The toughest and bravest of these groomsmen was the best man. Had women kidnapped men, they might have needed best women.

Where did the word *crap* come from? Does it have anything to do with shooting craps?

No, it derived from the first flush lavatory, Crapper's Valveless Water Waste Preventor, developed in 1837 by English sanitary engineer Thomas Crapper.

Is *gaga* short for a longer word?

Probably not. In French, *gaga* means a silly old man, and the meaning may simply have been modified. However, some think it is short for artist Paul Gauguin (1848–1903), who, it is said, revealed mental imbalance in his work.

Does the phrase *pin money* have anything to do with actual pins?

In its earliest use, it did mean the money to buy pins, the primary fasteners for clothing before buttons and zippers were invented. But by the sixteenth century, the phrase came to mean the money used for incidentals.

What is the origin of the word *hoodlum*?

There are several theories. One has to do with a gang of thugs in San Francisco led by a man named Muldoon. A fearful reporter, writing about him in 1877, spelled the name backward—Noodlum—and the compositor mistook the *N* for an *H*. A second theory claims the word is derived from the Pidgin English *hood lahnti*, meaning "very lazy mandarin." The final theory, which comes from San Francisco, says that the many Germans living in the city simply mispronounced the Bavarian word for hoodlum—*Hodalump*.

What is the origin of *attic*?

It comes from Attica in ancient Greece. There, an attic was a certain kind of low story above the main floor.

Over the centuries, however, *attic* has come to refer to any low space above the top floor of a building.

How did the dandelion get its name?

Not surprisingly, the name refers to a part of the lion. In England, before the sixteenth century, the weed was called lion's tooth because of its serrated leaf's resemblance to the lion's incisor. Later, the French translation—*dent de lion*—was adopted into English and eventually became anglicized to "dandelion."

What is the origin of the word *nightmare*?

It is named for a creature but not a horse. According to ancient superstition dating back to the eighth century in England, people thought a female monster or spirit—a so-called mare—would sit upon a sleeper's chest. This would cause a feeling of suffocation from which the sleeper would try to free himself, sometimes waking in the process.

Why are Oklahomans called Sooners?

According to Oklahoma history, it is in honor of the state's first settlers, who crossed the border into Oklahoma Territory *sooner* than the rest and obtained the choicest pieces of land. In 1889, Oklahoma Territory was opened for settlement, and the federal government attempted to close and police the borders until a designated time when a race would allow all new settlers to claim land. But the Sooners crossed the border early, upset the government's plans, and got the best land.

Where does the term *stark naked* come from?

It is a corruption of *start naked*. In the thirteenth century, when the phrase originated, *start* took the Anglo-Saxon form *steort*, which meant "tail" or "rump." Therefore, *stark naked* refers to someone naked to the tail.

What is the difference between *e.g.* and *i.e.?*

The abbreviation *e.g.*, standing for the Latin *exempli gratia*, or "for the sake of example," means exactly that—a series of examples: "large dogs, e.g., Saint Bernards and Great Danes." The abbreviation *i.e.*, standing for *id est*, or "that is," explains the subject you have mentioned: "large dogs, i.e., those over 3 feet tall and weighing over 50 pounds."

What is the difference between *et al.* and *et cetera*?

The Latin phrase *et al.*, short for *et alia* ("and other things") and *et alii* ("and other people"), is more specific than *et cetera* ("and the rest"). Only *et al.* can refer to people.

In mathematics, what is the difference between a *perimeter* and a *parameter*?

A *perimeter* is the distance around the boundary of a closed plane figure, such as a rectangle or circle. A *parameter* is a quantity that, when varied, affects the value of another quantity. Parameters are established to aid in determining an unknown figure.

What is the difference between a *median* and a *mean*?

A *median* is the point that divides a series of numbers so that half are on one side, half on the other. In the series 1, 4, 8, 20, 24, 27, 42, the median is 20. The *mean* is the average of a series, found by dividing the sum by the number of elements. In the series above, the mean (or average) is 18, or 126 divided by 7.

What is the difference between *semantics* and *semiotics*?

Semantics is the study of meaning. Approached from the philosophical point of view, it involves the relationships between words; approached from the linguistic point of view, it deals with changes in meaning over time. *Semiotics* is the study of signs and the use of signs in human communication.

What is the difference between *homographs*, *homophones*, and *homonyms*?

Homographs are two or more words that are spelled alike but have different meanings and sometimes different pronunciations, such as *lead* (the metal) and *lead* (to conduct).

Homophones are pronounced alike but have different spellings and meanings, such as *rite, right*, and *write*.

Homonyms are spelled or pronounced alike but have different meanings, such as *bowl* (the dish) and *bowl* (to take part in the game of bowling).

Where did the phrase *to eat humble pie* originate?

In the eighteenth century, the best meat of any meal went to the men of the house and their friends. The women and children ate the *umbles*—the tongue and entrails—baked in an *umble pie*. In time, the dish went out of fashion, but the phrase took on a new life that it still has today.

How did the expression *to make a bed* originate?

In the evening, citizens of the Roman Empire constructed their beds by placing straw into a cloth sack. The straw had to be emptied every night to dry; therefore, the beds had to be remade every night. This practice continued until the fifteenth century—in some countries, even later.

From what does the term *minutes of a meeting* derive?

Rather than measuring the time that passes during a meeting, the word *minutes* refers to the Latin *minutus*, or "small." This is because the occurrences of the meeting are meant to be noted shortly and quickly—not that the events themselves are unimportant.

What is the relation of *bedlam* to *Bethlehem*?

The word *bedlam*, now used to describe a scene of uproar and confusion, was originally a contraction of *Bethlehem*. It referred to Saint Mary of Bethlehem, a religious house in London that was converted into a hospital for the insane in 1402. The term came to mean a lunatic asylum, one of its inmates, or the type of environment one might expect inside.

Where does the word *salary* come from?

It evolved from *salarium argentium*, or "salt money," fees paid to Roman soldiers to buy the then precious commodity.

What is the origin of *kismet*?

From the Turkish *qismat*—"portion" or "lot"—it means fate or the completion of destiny.

Why is the practice of eating human flesh called cannibalism?

The practice, also called anthropophagy, is derived from the Spanish word for the Caribs, a West Indian tribe known for cannibalism.

What is the definition of everyone's favorite Scrabble word—*syzygy*?

The word is used by astronomers to describe the position of three bodies that are approximately in line. For example, when the moon is full, it is in syzygy with the earth and sun, because it is on the far side of the earth from the sun.

What is spelunking?

It is the exploration of caves as a hobby. It is not to be confused with speleology, the scientific study and exploration of caves.

Why are sweatshops called sweatshops?

It is not because the workers sweat a lot. In the 1840s in England, the word *sweating* meant the exaction of tedious work at low wages. The term *sweatshop*—a place where workers were "sweated"—was coined in the United States in 1867. Originally referring only to the garment industry, it was soon being applied to other businesses as well.

If the female side of a family is called the distaff side, what is the male side?

The spear side. A distaff was a stick with a cleft end, used to hold the flax or wool from which a woman spun thread. The distaff was considered a woman's tool, while the spear was a man's. Both ways of describing genealogy are now rarely used.

What is the difference between a boat and a ship?

The U.S. Navy defines a boat as "a vessel that can be hauled aboard a ship." In ordinary usage, however, large vessels are often called boats as well as ships.

What is the difference between a barrister and a solicitor?

Both types of professionals practice law in Great Britain, but their roles are different. A barrister represents clients in open court and may appear at the bar. A solicitor is allowed to conduct litigation in court but—with only a few exceptions—not to plead cases in open court. In practice, most plaintiffs and defendants deal with solicitors, not barristers.

What is the difference between a preface and a foreword?

At one time there was no difference: *Preface* was the Latinate term, *foreword* the Anglo-Saxon one, for a brief opening comment about a book's purpose. Now, many consider an author's introductory comment to be the preface, and anyone else's comment to be the foreword.

How deep is a fathom?
Six feet.

> *How far is a league?*
> It can vary from 2.4 to 4.6 miles.
>
> *What is the area of an acre?*
> 4,840 square yards, or 43,560 square feet.

Who invented the term *fifth column*?
A Fascist general named Gonzalo Queipo de Llano y Sierro is said to have coined the phrase during the Spanish Civil War (1936–1939). As four Fascist army columns closed in on Madrid, the general described his supporters inside the city as a "fifth column." The term came to mean any group of subversives trying to undermine a nation from within.

Is it permissible to split infinitives?
It depends on whom you ask. Some editors will still change "to boldly go where no man has gone before" to "to go boldly . . ." But other pundits now consider the taboo against split infinitives all but passé. The taboo

was introduced by eighteenth- and nineteenth-century grammarians for unknown reasons.

When should a writer use *insure* as opposed to *ensure*?

Writers should busy themselves with other things. *Insure* and *ensure* can be used interchangeably to mean "make certain." In the United States, however, the spelling *insure* is generally preferred to *ensure*, and only *insure* can be used to mean "indemnify against loss."

When should you use the word *irregardless*?

You should not. The word is redundant because the negative prefix *ir-* does the same work as the negative suffix *-less*. Use *regardless* instead.

Should you say, "Forgive us our trespasses, as we forgive *those* who trespass against us," or, as the English do, ". . . as we forgive *them* who trespass against us"?

Say it whichever way you like. The pronouns *those* and *them* are both correctly used as objects in this passage.

How did the word *ain't* become unacceptable?

The use of *ain't* as a substitute for *am not* or *are not* dates back to the reign of King Charles II—about 300 years. It is unclear how or why it became unacceptable.

How did the phrase *to 86* someone become popular?

The phrase, which generally means "put an end to," is said to have been part of a number code used in diners and soda fountains. In those early days, *86* meant "we're out of that dish," "don't serve that customer," or "don't serve another drink to that customer because he's already had too many." Over time, it has gained its more general meaning.

What is the origin of *to go scot free?*

In Old English, *scot* meant a payment, or one's share of a payment. *To go scot free* meant escaping that charge.

Why is a swan song a farewell?

According to ancient legend, it was thought that the swan, silent throughout its life, sang aloud in its final minutes.

How did the phrase *upside down* develop?

Believed to be an early form of *upsedown* or *up so down*, it came into popularity during the Elizabethan Age.

Why is the wolf a symbol of the troubles that must be kept from the door?

Throughout history, the wolf has been known for its insatiable appetite. This came to represent hunger and need.

Who passed the first buck?

The phrase *passing the buck* probably came into use in American poker games during the late nineteenth century. In 1872, Mark Twain wrote that players would pass an object—a buck—to remind them of who was to deal. It is also possible that *buck* is an old word for *bet*.

What was the original meaning of the phrase *to beat the band*?

The American expression, not more than a century old, referred to the aim of arriving at a parade site before the band passed.

What is the significance of *looking a gift horse in the mouth*?

The phrase, as old as the fourth century A.D., once had a literal meaning. Up to a certain number of years, a horse's age can be determined by examining its teeth. To perform such an examination on a horse you've been given is *looking a gift horse in the mouth*.

What is the derivation of *in like Flynn*?

The phrase is believed to have originated with Ed Flynn, head of New York City's Democratic party machine from 1922 to 1953. Flynn's political machine was always "in" power. The phrase gained further popularity in 1942, when swashbuckling actor Errol Flynn (1909–1959) was tried and acquitted on charges of the statutory rape of two teenage girls on his yacht.

Are there any words in the English language that use all five vowels?

Several, including *sequoia* and *facetious*.

When do the cows come home?

The old saying *waiting till the cows come home*—it is almost 400 years old—refers to the early-morning hour when cows line up at the farm gates, ready to be milked.

· 6 ·

FINE ARTS

◆◆◆◆◆

How old are the earliest musical instruments?
In the caves of France, archaeologists have found carved bones that appear to be wind and percussion instruments. These date from about 25,000 to 20,000 B.C.

When was the Nativity Scene first represented in art?
The scene of the newborn Christ, the Virgin Mary, and often shepherds and the Magi was first represented in the fourth century, carved on early Christian Roman sarcophagi.

Do gargoyles have a practical function?
The grotesque statues that decorate medieval cathedrals—and the medieval-influenced architecture of some universities—are not merely decorative. A gargoyle is technically a waterspout that projects from a

roof gutter to throw rainwater clear of a building. The term is applied more loosely to any grotesquely carved figure.

What was Botticelli's real name?

Alessandro di Mariano Filipepi (c. 1444–1510). The Florentine painter's nickname, Botticelli, meant "little barrel" and was presumably a reference to his girth.

How long did it take Leonardo da Vinci to paint the *Mona Lisa*? Who was the model?

It took Leonardo four years (1503–1507)—long enough for his patron, Francesco del Giocondo, to get impatient. Giocondo had commissioned the portrait of his third wife, Lisa, but enough was enough. Giocondo refused to pay for the unfinished portrait, and Leonardo sold it to the king of France instead. This is the traditional tale—but it is based on sparse evidence.

How did El Greco sign his paintings?

As Doménikos Theotokópoulos, his real name. The artist (c. 1541–1614) wrote the name in Greek characters, sometimes followed by *Kres* for "Cretan"—his national origin.

How many people can be seated in Saint Peter's Basilica?

Begun in 1526 and completed in 1626, it accommodates 50,000—a little less than Yankee Stadium, which seats 57,545.

Which of the fine arts features a work called *The Rake's Progress*, and who is responsible for it?

Actually, both art and music lay claim to a rake's progress. The English artist William Hogarth began a series of eight satirical paintings entitled *The Rake's Progress* in 1732. Hogarth engraved the series three years later. In the twentieth century, Igor Stravinsky wrote a three-act opera called *The Rake's Progress*, his last neoclassical work. Based on the Hogarth series, with a libretto by W. H. Auden and Chester Kallman, the opera was first performed on September 11, 1951, in Venice.

What is the difference between baroque and rococo?

The baroque style dominated European art in the seventeenth century. To an art historian, it connotes vigorous movement, emotional intensity, and a sense of balance (*not* art that is excessive and florid—the popular meaning of the word *baroque*). The rococo style flourished in the eighteenth century, after the baroque period; it is characterized by lightness, grace, and playfulness. The word *rococo* was coined by merging the Italian *barocco* (baroque) and the French *rocaille* (originally a term for fancy rock- and shellwork).

What is the meaning of the art term *picturesque*?

It is a style of landscape painting that flourished in the late eighteenth and early nineteenth centuries. Picturesque landscapes were somewhere between the beautiful and the sublime—not serene, not awe-inspiring, but irregular, pleasing to the eye, and full of interesting detail. Picturesque painters included the Englishman Thomas Girtin and the Frenchman Gaspard Dughet. The movement represents a stage between neoclassical regularity and Romantic passion.

How did the members of the Pre-Raphaelite Brotherhood sign their paintings?

The members of the secret brotherhood formed in 1848 exhibited their paintings anonymously with the signature *PRB*. The founding members were Dante Gabriel Rossetti, William Holman Hunt, and John Everett Millais, who were rebelling against the unimaginative academic art of their day. Though the PRB (unmasked in 1850) had a profound influence on Western painting, it lasted as an organization for only about 10 years.

What is the formal name of the painting known as *Whistler's Mother*?

Arrangement in Gray and Black: Portrait of the Painter's Mother, by James Abbott McNeill Whistler, 1872.

When did the tango originate?

The modern ballroom tango appeared about 1880 in Argentina. It combined the old tango of Spain—a light-spirited variety of flamenco—with the *milonga*, a fast, hot Argentine dance. At first considered low-class, the new tango was all the rage in fashionable circles by 1915.

Is anyone credited with writing "Chopsticks"?

Arthur de Lulli is named as the writer of the 1877 piano exercise. The name is actually a pseudonym for a sixteen-year-old girl named Euphemia Allen.

Where was Tin Pan Alley?

The birthplace of much of twentieth-century popular music, where songwriters plied their trade, actually had two locations—both in New York City. The first Tin Pan Alley section sprang up around Fourteenth Street; the second was in the Times Square area.

Where does the name Dada come from?

The name for this artistic movement—founded in Zurich in 1915 as a revolt against complacent art—is drawn not from an artist or a technique but from the child's word for a parent, *dada*—which in French, curiously, also means "hobbyhorse." Whatever its origin, the name Dada is intended to be devoid of meaning. As one of the movement's founders, poet Tristan Tzara (1896–1963), claimed, "Like everything in life, Dada is useless."

What is the 12-tone theory in music?

It is music based on the serial ordering of all 12 pitches on the chromatic scale—the scale that includes both the black and white keys on the piano. (The diatonic scale of seven pitches includes only the white keys.) In the 12-tone system—developed by Austro-Hungarian composer Arnold Schoenberg (1874–1951) in the early 1920s—the composer decides on a series of all 12 pitches placed in any order. That order becomes the basis for the entire composition.

Where did Art Deco get its name?

From the Exposition Internationale des Arts Décoratifs et Industriels Modernes in Paris in 1925. It became the dominant style of architecture and interior design in the 1920s and 1930s.

What is a bolero and what does Ravel have to do with it?

A bolero is a lively Spanish dance in 3/4 time with a strongly marked rhythm. The dancers perform intricate steps while keeping time with castanets. Maurice Ravel published a well-known orchestral version of the dance—*Bolero*—in 1928. A bolero is also a short jacket, perhaps first worn during performances of the dance.

When did Alexander Calder make his first mobile?

He made his first unpowered mobiles in 1934—pieces of tin suspended on thin wires or cords, and responding to the faintest air currents. But before then, beginning in 1931, he had made constructions activated by hand or by motor power. These became known as mobiles, while Calder's nonmoving constructions became known as stabiles.

What is the blue note?

It is a musical note—usually a flatted third or seventh—that gives a blues feeling to a song. The Blue Note is also the name of a popular nightclub in New York's Greenwich Village.

What is the most famous auto-destructive work of art?

Probably Swiss sculptor Jean Tinguely's *Homage to New York*, which blew itself up at the Museum of Modern Art in 1960. The work was meant to satirize modern technological civilization. Constructed of an old piano and other junk, the piece failed to operate as planned and caused a fire, witnessed by a distinguished audience.

In opera parlance, what is the difference between a diva and a prima donna?

A prima donna is simply the leading lady of an opera company. A diva, a "goddess," is a legendary or highly celebrated leading lady.

Is Mount Rushmore the largest sculpture in the world?

No. The prize goes to the sculpture of Jefferson Davis, Robert E. Lee, and Thomas ("Stonewall") Jackson that covers 1.33 acres on the face of Stone Mountain near Atlanta, Georgia. It was created between September 12, 1963, and March 3, 1972.

◆ 7 ◆

THE FIRST

◆◆◆◆◆

Where was the first house of prostitution?

The first such house on record may have been Ka-Kum, located in the city of Erech (or Uruk) in Sumer and dating back to about 3000 B.C. The first brothels in Europe were located in Athens about 600 B.C. These nonprofit operations sanctioned by the leader Solon charged men 1 cent per visit.

What was the first personal ad?

It might well have been a matrimonial advertisement that appeared in a British publication called the *Collection for the Improvement of Husbandry and Trade* on July 19, 1695. The ad read:

> A Gentleman about 30 Years of Age, that says he has a Very Good Estate, would willingly Match Himself to some young Gentlewoman that has a fortune of £3,000 or thereabouts, And he will make Settlement to Content.

Even in this first ad, youth and money were prerequisites.

What was the first restaurant?

While meals had long been offered in taverns, cookshops, and coffeehouses, the first place known as a restaurant was the Champ d'Oiseau, which opened in Paris in 1765. At the entrance was the Latin motto *Venite ad me, omne qui stomacho laboratis, et ego restaurabo vos*, or "Come to me, anybody whose stomach groans, and I will restore you."

When was the first public opinion poll taken?

To assess voters' preferences in the 1824 presidential election, citizens were asked whom they preferred. The results, published in the *Harrisburg Pennsylvanian* on July 24, 1824, gave Andrew Jackson a commanding lead over John Quincy Adams and all others. However, Adams won the election.

What was the first monopoly in the United States?

It is considered to have been John Jacob Astor's American Fur Company, which made him the wealthiest person in the United States and allowed him to found the Astor Library, one of the cornerstones of the New York Public Library.

When was the first department store built?

In 1848, the Marble Dry Goods Palace opened on Broadway in New York City. Its proprietor and developer was Alexander Turney Stewart, formerly a schoolmaster in Ireland. By the time of his death in 1876, the blocklong store yielded annual earnings of $70 million.

What was the first zoo in the United States?

It was the Philadelphia Zoological Gardens, which opened in 1874. In 1938, it became the site of the first children's zoo. Founded and operated by the Zoological Society of Philadelphia, the Philadelphia Zoo currently houses more than 1,400 specimens of over 400 species.

What was the first skyscraper?

It was the 10-story Home Insurance Company Building in Chicago, designed by William Le Baron Jenney and completed in 1885. The first tall building to be supported by an internal frame of iron and steel rather than by thick masonry walls, it was demolished in 1931.

Who was the first black U.S. senator?

Hiram Revels (1822–1901) of Mississippi became the first black senator on February 25, 1870. He completed the term begun by Jefferson Davis, who had resigned to become the president of the Confederacy. Aside from Blanche K. Bruce, who represented Mississippi from 1875 to 1881, there were no other black senators until 1966, when Edward Brooke, a Republican from Massachusetts, took office.

Who was the first black mayor?

Carl B. Stokes (b. 1927), great-grandson of a slave, who was mayor of Cleveland from 1967 to 1971.

Who was the first black U.S. general?

It was Benjamin O. Davis, Sr. (1877–1970), promoted to the rank of brigadier general in the U.S. Army in 1940.

Who was the first female general in the U.S. armed forces?

Elizabeth P. Hoisington, who was appointed to the post of director of the Women's Army Corps in June 1970.

Who was the first woman to be commemorated on a U.S. postage stamp?

It was the wife of the first president, and it did not happen until the twentieth century. In 1901, Martha Washington was commemorated on the 8-cent stamp. In 1918, she was pictured on the 2-cent prepaid postcard; in 1920, on the 4-cent stamp; and in 1938, on the 1½-cent stamp.

Who was the first man to die in the electric chair?

Convicted axe-murderer William Kemmler became the first man to be executed by electrocution on August 6, 1890, at Auburn State Prison, New York. Harold P. Brown had conceived the idea of death by electrocution and conducted the early experiments; Thomas

Alva Edison supplied the equipment. According to the official report, the procedure, which had to be repeated to induce death, took eight minutes.

Who was the first person to die in the gas chamber?

Gee Jon, convicted of assassinating a member of a rival Chinese tong, died in a gas chamber in Nevada State Prison in Carson City on February 8, 1924. The idea of the gas chamber was introduced by Major D. A. Turner of the U.S. Army Medical Corps as the "quickest and most humane method of putting a human to death." The process, which used hydrocyanic gas, took six minutes.

Where was the first used-car dealership?

It was the Motor Car Company of London, which opened in September 1897. It offered 17 secondhand vehicles, ranging in price from £30 to £335.

What was the first stolen car?

It was a Peugeot, owned by Baron de Zuylen of France and stolen in June 1896 by a mechanic from the manufacturer's plant in Paris, where it had been taken for repairs.

What was the first movie theater in the United States?

On June 26, 1896, the 400-seat Vitascope Hall was opened at the corner of Canal Street and Exchange Place in New Orleans by William T. Rock. For 10 cents, viewers could peer into the projection room; for another 10 cents, they could see the Edison Vitascope projector. A popular film of the time was *May Irwin Kiss*, one of the first movies to portray any form of on-screen sex.

What was the first drive-in movie?

A 10-acre site in Camden, New Jersey, was opened by Richard Hollingshead on June 6, 1933. The screen measured 40 by 30 feet; there was room for 400 cars.

What was the first coast-to-coast highway?

The Lincoln Highway was the first coast-to-coast paved road in the United States. Opened in 1913, it ran from New York to California.

What was the first passenger airline?

The Saint Petersburg–Tampa Airboat Line of Saint Petersburg, Florida, began flight operations on January 1, 1914. The twice-a-day service took passengers one at a time across 20-mile-wide Tampa Bay. The complete trip in a Benoit flying boat covered 36 miles and cost $5. The service ran for four months.

When were airplanes first used by the U.S. armed forces?

They were used unsuccessfully in 1916 against Pancho Villa in Mexico. In 1917, the First Aero Squadron, the first air unit, fought in World War I.

Who made the first transatlantic flight?

Albert C. ("Putty") Read and crew aboard the *Lame Duck*, May 16 to 27, 1919. They flew, with stops, from Trespassey Bay, Canada, to Plymouth, England. The first nonstop flight was that of John William Alcock and Arthur Whitten Brown, June 14 to 15, 1919. Charles Lindbergh's 1927 flight, May 20 to 21, was the first *solo* transatlantic flight.

When did the first radio station broadcast?

On November 2, 1920, KDKA in East Pittsburgh, Pennsylvania, broadcast for the first time. Its initial newscast reported that Warren Harding had been elected president of the United States.

What were the first frozen foods?

The first line of Birds Eye products, launched in the mid-1920s and named for their inventor, Clarence Birdseye, included individually packaged boxes of peas, spinach, berries, cherries, fish, and meats. Birdseye had investigated the preservation of foods by ice while on U.S. government surveys of fish and wildlife in Labrador in 1912 and 1915. During the winter, he wrote, "I saw natives catching fish in fifty below zero weather, which froze stiff as soon as they were taken out of the water. Months later, when they were thawed out, some of those fish were still alive."

Who was the first Hollywood star to place his or her footprints at Grauman's Chinese Theatre?

Silent-picture actress Norma Talmadge (1897–1957) started the tradition when she accidentally stumbled onto a freshly laid cement sidewalk in front of the theater in 1927.

What was the first television news-broadcast?

The first news event to be televised was the nomination of Alfred E. Smith for the presidency in Albany, New York, on August 22, 1928. The program was transmitted by Schenectady's WGY. The first regular news reports were 15-minute daily programs transmitted over New York's WCBS and WNBT, beginning on July 1, 1941.

When was the first blood bank opened?

Not until 1940 in New York City. It was designed and operated by American surgeon Richard Charles Drew (1904–1950), who, because he was black, could not contribute blood to the bank.

Where and when was the world's first shopping center built?

The first urban one was Roland Park Shopping Center, built in 1896 in Baltimore, Maryland. The first suburban shopping center was built in 1928 in Ardmore, Pennsylvania. Called Suburban Square, it offered two department stores, doctors' offices, a movie theater, and 17 other shops.

When was the first laundromat opened?

On April 18, 1934, the Washateria in Fort Worth, Texas, was opened by J. F. Cantrell. It offered four electric washing machines that were rented by the hour.

What was the first spacecraft to land on the moon?
Luna 2, launched by the USSR on September 12, 1959, crash-landed between the craters Archimedes and Autolycus in the Mare Imbrium on September 14. A successful landing was made by *Luna 9* on February 3, 1966.

Who was the first woman in space?
Valentina V. Tereshkova of the USSR. She made 48 orbits of the earth in a three-day mission in *Vostok 6*, June 16 to 19, 1963.

Who was the first female to hold a post in the U.S. Cabinet?
It was Frances Perkins, who served as Secretary of Labor under Franklin D. Roosevelt from 1933 to 1945.

Who were the first women to head the two major political parties in the United States?
In 1972, Jean Westwood became the first to head the Democratic party; in 1974, Mary Louise Smith became the first to head the Republican party.

♦ 8 ♦

GEOGRAPHY

♦♦♦♦♦

How did Europe get its name?

Though its origin is not known for certain, the name is very old. A Greek hymn to Apollo from the sixth century B.C. mentions the name, which originally applied only to part of the Balkan Peninsula. *Europe* probably derives from a word meaning "mainland," though it may be related to the Assyrian *ereb*—"darkness, west," and therefore "land of the setting sun."

Where did Asia get its name?

Probably from the Assyrian *asu*—"sunrise, east." *Asu* originally referred only to the east coast of the Aegean Sea but gradually came to include the whole continent.

Where was Troy?

Troy was located in present-day Turkey at the mound now called Hissarlik, about 4 miles from the mouth of the Dardanelles. Also known as Ilium—hence the

Greek epic set during the Trojan War is called *The Iliad*—Troy was destroyed at the end of that war (c. 1200 B.C.). It was first excavated by Heinrich Schliemann in 1871.

How large was Troy?

What Homer referred to as "wind-swept Troy" was not what we would call a great city. It was a village of some 7 acres.

Where was Byzantium?

This ancient Greek city was on the shores of the Bosporus. It was renamed Constantinople when the Emperor Constantine moved the Roman capital there in A.D. 330; it became the seat of the Byzantine (or Eastern) Roman Empire. It is now called Instanbul and is one of the most commonly known cities in Turkey.

Why is Persia now called Iran?

The people of this country in southwestern Asia always called their homeland Iran, or "Land of the Aryans." But Westerners started calling it Persia in the sixth century B.C.—taking the name from Persis, or Parsa (modern Fārs), a region of southern Iran. In 1935, the country's government officially requested that the nation be referred to as Iran.

How many continents are there?

In the traditional list, there are seven: Africa, Antarctica, Asia, Australia, Europe, North America, and

South America. However, Europe and Asia are sometimes considered a single continent, Eurasia—making only six. Asia is the largest continent, comprising about 17 million square miles. Australia is the smallest, comprising only about 3 million square miles.

What are the five largest lakes?

1. *Kaspiyskoye More* (*or Caspian Sea*). USSR–Iran
2. *Superior*. United States–Canada
3. *Victoria*. Tanzania–Uganda–Kenya
4. *Aralskoye More* (*or Aral Sea*). USSR
5. *Huron*. United States–Canada

How thick is the ice that covers Antarctica?

The continent is almost completely covered with an ice sheet about 6,500 feet thick.

How much of the earth's surface is permanently frozen?

About 20 percent of the earth is under permafrost. This means it has had a temperature below 32 degrees Fahrenheit for over two years. In Siberia, some sections of land are frozen to depths of 5,000 feet.

How much of the earth is unexplored?

What is left is approximately 140 million square miles of ocean floor, equal to two and a half times the surface area of the earth's islands and continents.

What islands are part of the Antilles?

The islands of this main chain of Caribbean islands are divided into two groups—the Greater Antilles and the Lesser Antilles. The islands of the Greater Antilles are: Cuba, Jamaica, Hispaniola (Haiti and the Dominican Republic), and Puerto Rico. Those of the Lesser Antilles are: the Virgin Islands, the Leeward Islands, the Windward Islands, Barbados, Trinidad and Tobago, Curaçao, and Margarita. (The Leeward Islands include Antigua and Guadeloupe; the Windward Islands include Martinique and Grenada; the Virgin Islands include Saint Thomas and Saint Croix.) The Bahamas are not part of the Antilles.

When did Great Britain become the United Kingdom?

The United Kingdom of Great Britain was formed in 1707, when England, Scotland, and Wales were united by the Act of Union. But the United Kingdom of Great Britain and Ireland was not formed until 1801. In 1945—24 years after most of Ireland had won its independence—Great Britain's official name became the United Kingdom of Great Britain and Northern Ireland.

What's the smallest country on earth?

It is Vatican City, the seat of the Roman Catholic Church in Rome. At 0.16 square mile, it is less than half the size of the next smallest country, Monaco (0.4 square mile). Vatican City became an independent country in 1929. Its 750 inhabitants are ruled by the pope and a committee of three cardinals.

Where was Bohemia? How did it become associated with a bohemian lifestyle?

Founded in the tenth century, the kingdom of Bohemia was located in what is now Czechoslovakia. From 1526 to 1914, it was ruled by the Hapsburg princes of Austria. At the end of World War I, the Czechs of Bohemia and Moravia joined with the Slovaks of Slovakia to form the new Republic of Czechoslovakia.

In the nineteenth century, artists and other vagabonds became known as bohemians because the French believed that Bohemia was the homeland of the Gypsies. Artists were held to live a Gypsy-like, or bohemian, life.

How was California named?

In 1535, the sight of what is now Baja California in Mexico evoked for Spanish conquistador Hernán Cortés an imaginary island and its female black ruler, Calafía, in a popular Spanish novel. In September 1542, when Spanish explorer Juan Rodríguez Cabrillo stepped onshore from San Diego Bay, the entire Pacific coast had been named California.

Which U.S. state is known as the Land of Steady Habits?

Connecticut.

The Blue Hen State?
Delaware.

The Gopher State?
Minnesota.

The Beaver State?
Oregon.

Which U.S. city is known as the Pittsburgh of the South?
Birmingham, Alabama.

The Rubber Capital of the World?
Akron, Ohio.

Pretzel City?
Reading, Pennsylvania.

Insurance City?
Hartford, Connecticut.

Cement City?
Allentown, Pennsylvania.

Celery City?
Kalamazoo, Michigan.

How many islands are part of the Hawaiian Islands?
There are 132 islands. The eight main islands are: Hawaii, Kahoolawe, Maui, Lanai, Molokai, Oahu, Kauai, and Niihau. The islands are spread over 1,500 square miles.

What determines where the Arctic Circle lies?
The Arctic Circle lies at 66°30′ north latitude, because that is the southernmost latitude where the sun can be

seen for a full 24-hour period on or about June 22, the first day of summer (summer solstice). On the same day in the Antarctic Circle (south of 66°30′ south latitude), the sun does not shine at all. The situation is reversed during the winter solstice.

Where is the Pole of Inaccessibility?

It is the point on the continent of Antarctica farthest in all directions from the seas that surround it. The site lies on the Polar Plateau and is occupied by a Soviet meteorological research station. The term *Pole of Inaccessibility* is also sometimes used to describe the point in the Arctic Ocean equidistant from the surrounding landmasses, about 400 miles from the North Pole.

What are the Seven Hills of Rome?

These are the hills on or about which Rome was built. The original city was built on the Palatine Hill. The other six hills are: the Capitoline, Quirinal, Viminal, Esquiline, Caelian, and Aventine.

Where is the largest Chinese settlement outside the Orient?

San Francisco's Chinatown district. It covers only about 12 square blocks.

What is the longest bridge in the world?

The Humber suspension bridge over the Humber River near Hull, England. Completed in 1981, it is 4,626 feet long. The Verrazano-Narrows Bridge in New York City—the world's second-largest bridge—is

4,260 feet long. The Golden Gate Bridge in San Francisco is third, at 4,200 feet.

How many time zones are there in North America?

Eight. From east to west, they are: Newfoundland, Atlantic, Eastern, Central, Mountain, Pacific, Yukon, and Alaskan. When it's 9:00 A.M. in Newfoundland, it's only 2:00 A.M. in Alaska.

What is the international date line?

It is the 180th meridian of longitude, marking the point where one civil day ends and another begins. It runs north and south across the middle of the Pacific Ocean. In some places it veers a little to avoid lopping off parts of geographical locations such as Siberia.

> *Which way do you have to go to gain a day?*
> If you go west to east—for example, from Japan to California—you gain a day: Tuesday becomes Monday. Go the other way and Monday becomes Tuesday.

Where is the Mosquito Coast?

The Spanish Costa de Mosquitos is a 40-mile-wide band along the coasts of Nicaragua and Honduras. It follows the Caribbean Sea for about 225 miles.

What countries are situated on the Balkan Peninsula?

Albania, Bulgaria, Greece, Romania, Turkey, and Yugoslavia are all located wholly or in part on the peninsula, which lies between the Adriatic Sea and the Black Sea. The Balkan Peninsula is one of the three great peninsulas of southern Europe—the others being the Iberian and the Italian.

How many republics are in the Union of Soviet Socialist Republics?

The USSR is composed of 15 republics:

Armenia	Lithuania
Azerbaijan	Moldavia
Belorussia	Russian Soviet Federated
Estonia	Socialist Republic (RSFSR)
Georgia	Tadzhikistan
Kazakhstan	Turkmenistan
Kirghizia	Ukraine
Latvia	Uzbekistan

Where is the Rock of Gibraltar and what country owns it?

Gibraltar is a limestone promontory off the southeastern coast of Spain. Connected to Spain by an isthmus, it commands the northeastern entrance to the Strait of Gibraltar, which joins the Atlantic Ocean and the Mediterranean Sea. Gibraltar is a self-governing British colony.

How long is the Grand Canyon?

The gorge of the Colorado River is 217 miles long. Fifty-six miles lie within Grand Canyon National Park in Arizona. The canyon varies in width from 4 to 18 miles.

How large is the Silicon Valley?

The stretch between San Jose and San Francisco runs 55 miles.

Where is the Dinosaur National Monument?

The nearly 205,000 acres of dinosaur beds are located in Colorado and Utah.

Does the United States have any territory in Cuba?

Yes—about 36,000 acres. The United States has a naval base at Guantánamo Bay near the western end of the south coast of Cuba, 572 miles from Havana. The United States has leased the site since 1903—despite pressure from Fidel Castro's government to leave.

How large is Luxembourg?

The tiny country—known as a Grand Duchy since 1815—covers 998 square miles, an area slightly smaller than Rhode Island. Its 1980 population was about 350,000. It is sandwiched between Belgium, France, and West Germany.

What are the United Arab Emirates?

They are a federation of seven Arab states on the Persian Gulf: Abu Dhabi, Ajman, Dubai, Fujairah, Ras al-Khaimah, Sharjah, and Umm al-Qaiwain. Independent since 1971, they should be distinguished from the

United Arab Republic, which was formed when Egypt and Syria united in 1958. Syria seceded from the union in 1961, but the name United Arab Republic stuck with Egypt. Egypt was renamed the Arab Republic of Egypt in 1972.

How many geographic locations have been named for Queen Victoria?

There are eight:

> *Victoria, Australia*. The smallest, most densely populated state in Australia.
> *Victoria, British Columbia, Canada*. The largest city on Vancouver Island.
> *Victoria Falls*. On the Zambezi River at the borders of Zambia and Zimbabwe.
> *Victoria Island*. A large island in the Arctic Ocean off northern Canada.
> *Lake Victoria*. The largest lake in Africa, also known as Victoria Nyanza, located on the borders of Uganda and Tanzania.
> *Victoria Land, Antarctica*. A row of mountains.
> *Victoria Nile*. Part of the White Nile, located in Uganda.
> *Victoriaville, Quebec, Canada*. A town in the province of Quebec.

Where was Sherwood Forest?

The royal hunting ground frequented by Robin Hood and his merry men was located in Nottinghamshire,

England. Today Sherwood Forest is under the protection of the British Forestry Commission.

Where is Tipperary?

It is a county in Munster Province, Ireland, occupying a broad strip of land between the Shannon and Suir rivers. The Irish name for Tipperary is Contae Tiobraid Árann. It *is* a long way from most places.

◆ 9 ◆

HOLIDAYS

◆◆◆◆

What does *auld lang syne* mean?

In Scottish it means literally "old long ago."

What day was observed as Adam and Eve Day on the medieval church calendar?

Christmas Eve—December 24. One element has survived from the medieval plays put on that day depicting Adam and Eve's fall: the paradise tree, representing the tree that bore the forbidden fruit. The paradise tree, set up in many German households by 1561, was the forerunner of the modern Christmas tree.

What holiday is associated with the Lord of Misrule?

Christmas. In medieval England, the Lord of Misrule was the leader of Christmas revelries.

How many gifts would you have if you received all the gifts mentioned in the song "The Twelve Days of Christmas"?

364.

Why is Groundhog Day observed in February?

Because of latitude. German immigrants to Punxsutawney, Pennsylvania, brought an older version of Groundhog Day to America—one in which badgers predict the weather. The immigrants discovered that, in the United States, groundhogs are easier to find. At the latitude of Punxsutawney, a groundhog emerges from hibernation in February.

How accurate are groundhogs at predicting the weather?

Over a 60-year period, groundhogs have been only 28 percent accurate in guessing when spring will start. This may be because their staying out of their burrows or rushing back into them has more to do with sexual desire or hunger than with weather or shadows.

What significance does February 2 have for Christians?

It is more than Groundhog Day—it is Candlemas, which commemorates the presentation of Jesus in the Temple. Candles are blessed and carried in a procession. In England, the feast is associated with Groundhog Day: If the weather is sunny on Candlemas, winter will remain; if cloudy, spring will come.

When is George Washington's birthday?

For the first 19 years of his life, George Washington (born in 1731) celebrated his birthday on February 11. After the British parliament replaced the Julian calendar with the Gregorian calendar (in 1752), Washington celebrated his birthday 11 days later—on February 22.

How is the date for Easter Sunday determined each year?

Easter Sunday always falls on the first Sunday after the first full moon after March 21, the vernal equinox. The holiday can occur any time between March 22 and April 25.

When is Arbor Day? When was it first observed?

This holiday for planting trees was first observed on April 10, 1872, in Nebraska. It is now usually observed on the last Friday in April.

When did May Day, May 1, become an international day for honoring workers?

The observance of May Day as a workers' holiday began in 1890 in Europe, in support of laborers' demands for an eight-hour working day in the United States. The Soviet Union made it a national holiday, and it is observed as such in Socialist and Communist countries.

Who originated Mother's Day?

Julia Ward Howe, women's suffrage leader and author of "The Battle Hymn of the Republic," made the first known suggestion for Mother's Day in 1872. She saw it as a day dedicated to peace, to be celebrated on June 2. But it was Anna Jarvis of Grafton, West Virginia, who, in 1907, began campaigning for nationwide observance of Mother's Day on the second Sunday in May. In 1915, President Woodrow Wilson proclaimed Mother's Day as an annual national observance.

What day is called Independence Day in the following countries?

> *Burma.* January 4 (1948)
> *Greece.* March 25 (1821)
> *Cuba.* May 20 (1902)
> *Nigeria.* October 1 (1960)
> *Lebanon.* November 22 (1943)

When was Thanksgiving made a national holiday?

In 1863, after a concerted campaign by ladies' magazine editor Sarah Josepha Hale. That year, President Abraham Lincoln officially proclaimed Thanksgiving a national holiday, to be held on the last Thursday of November. In 1939, to stimulate the Depression economy, President Franklin D. Roosevelt moved the date of Thanksgiving up one week. After two years of public protest, Congress passed a law establishing the fourth Thursday in November as the official Thanksgiving.

Why is the word *Christmas* abbreviated as *Xmas?*

Because the Greek letter *x* is the first letter of the Greek word for Christ, *Xristos*. The word *Xmas*, meaning

"Christ's Mass," was commonly used in Europe by the sixteenth century. It was not an attempt to take *Christ* out of *Christmas*.

What is the earliest reference to Christmas's being celebrated on December 25?

In the middle of the second century, Christians in Antioch were already celebrating Christ's birth on that day. The day was not officially recognized by the Church as the date of Christ's birth until A.D. 350.

> *Why December 25?*
> The day was formerly celebrated by worshippers of the god Mithra as the *Dies Invicti Solis*, or "Day of the Invincible Sun." It seemed natural to Christians to replace Mithra with Christ—called in the Bible the Sun of Righteousness.

What do they observe in China on December 25?

In the Republic of China—Taiwan—they observe Constitution Day, a national holiday.

When did trees become part of Christmas celebrations?

Evergreen trees and wreaths have been used as symbols of eternal life since the ancient times of the Egyptians, Chinese, and Hebrews. After the coming of Christianity, evergreens were still used in Scandinavia—to scare away the devil. In the Middle Ages, the Christmas tree, decorated with candles and wafers (symbols of Christ and the Host), became popular, as did the gaily decorated wooden Christmas pyramid. By the sixteenth century, the two objects merged into what we now know as the Christmas tree. By the nineteenth century, the Christmas tree was popular across Europe and the United States.

How old is Hanukkah?

It was first celebrated in 165 B.C.

> #### What does the word mean?
> Rededication. It refers to the cleansing and re-dedication of the Temple in Jerusalem by the Maccabees after defeating their Syrian-Greek oppressors.

Do Jews around the world display menorahs in their windows during the Hanukkah season?

No. The menorah—the nine-branched candelabrum—is a traditional symbol of Hanukkah, but displaying it in the window is largely an American custom.

What is the name of Santa's brother?

According to Pennsylvania Dutch and French tradition, he is Bells Nichols. He visits every home on New Year's Eve after the children are asleep, and if plates are set out for him, he fills them with cakes and cookies.

· 10 ·

THE HUMAN BODY

◆◆◆◆◆

What is the largest number of fingers and toes ever possessed by one person?
On September 16, 1921, a baby boy in Shoreditch, East London, England, was reported to have been born with 14 fingers and 15 toes.

What is the longest recorded attack of hiccuping? Of sneezing? Of yawning?
The longest hiccuping attack lasted 65 years; the longest sneezing fit lasted 978 days; the longest yawning ordeal took five weeks.

How many square feet of skin cover the human body?
The average body has 14 to 18 square feet of skin.

How much of the body is made up of bones?
Strong and light, the skeleton of the average person accounts for less than 20 percent of body weight.

How much of the average body is muscle?
Most men's bodies are composed of about 40 percent muscle; women's bodies are 30 percent muscle.

How many hairs are on a human head?
About 100,000.

> *How fast do they grow?*
> About 0.01 inch every day.

How much hair does an average person lose each day?
Whether the person is male or female, the number is the same—about 25 to 125 hairs. These are replaced by new hairs—unless the person starts balding.

What causes balding?
Balding occurs when hair follicles shrink and become less productive. Instead of the new hairs being cultivated to replace the ones that fall out naturally each day, they are allowed to remain embryonic—at the most, in a light, peach-fuzz stage. Probably some hormonal action triggers the follicles to behave this way, but it is not known what causes that hormonal action—only that sex, age, and heredity appear to be involved.

How many times does a heart beat in a lifetime?
Assuming that the heart beats at least once a second, by the time a person is 70, his or her heart will have beat at least 2.8 billion times.

Where did the part of the throat known as the Adam's apple get its name?

The Adam's apple refers to a legend that claims a piece of the forbidden fruit stuck in Adam's throat. This part of the throat is actually a projection of the thyroid cartilage of the larynx.

What is the apple of one's eye?

It is the pupil, which was likened to an apple because, in the ninth century, it was believed to be a solid round mass.

What happens when a part of one's body "falls asleep"?

The sensation, called neurapraxia, usually occurs when a nerve is compressed between a bone and another hard object. Blood continues to circulate through the affected area.

What part of the brain is Broca's area?

Broca's area is the part of the brain associated with motor control of speech. It is usually located in the left but sometimes in the right inferior frontal convolution. It is named for its discoverer, the nineteenth-century French surgeon Paul Broca.

How many sperm cells are contained in an average human ejaculation?

About 200 million to 300 million. Yet sperm cells make up only 2 to 5 percent of total sperm volume; the rest is composed of fluids, known as seminal plasma, that help keep the sperm cells alive.

When does a human embryo have its first heartbeat?

At the age of three weeks, when the heart of the embryo looks like a tube. As it begins to beat, it starts the blood circulating through the few blood vessels that have formed around it.

Is there any bone in the body that does not connect with other bones?

The hyoid bone resides by itself in the throat. It supports the tongue and its muscles.

Do identical twins have the same fingerprints?

No.

Do fingerprints have a function?

They provide traction for your fingers, helping you to grasp things.

When does a fetus acquire fingerprints?

At the age of three months.

Why do we get goose bumps when it's cold?

Goose bumps are a vestige from the days when humans were covered with hair. When it got cold, the hairs stood on end, creating a trap for air and providing insulation. The hairs have long since disappeared, but in the places where they used to be, the skin still bristles, trying to get warm.

How does a knockout punch knock someone out?
A knockout punch causes a chain reaction in the victim's circulatory system. The supply of blood pools in the abdomen, reducing circulation to the brain—and resulting in loss of consciousness.

How much water does a person drink in a lifetime?
About 16,000 gallons.

How long are the intestines?
The small intestine, which is contained in the central and lower abdominal cavity, is 20 to 23 feet long. The large intestine is 5 feet long.

Can a person with long-term constipation be poisoned by his own wastes?
No. There are several cases on record in which fecal material has been stored in the bowels for over a year without causing any ill effects—aside from the discomfort of carrying around an extra 60 to 100 pounds of weight.

What's the difference between a gamete and a zygote?
A gamete is a mature, functional sex cell (i.e., an egg or sperm) that can unite with a gamete of the opposite sex. A zygote is what results when the two gametes fuse.

Is there a gluteus minimus?
Yes. There are three gluteus muscles—the large, fleshy muscles of the buttocks that connect the hipbone (the

pelvic girdle) and the thighbone (the femur). The gluteus maximus is the muscle at the surface of the buttocks, below which is the gluteus medius. The gluteus minimus is below that.

How much is the human body worth?

Newspaper columnists and others have claimed that the body's chemical worth is between 98 cents and $5. But one doctor argues that, at the rates currently charged by large chemical distributors, the body's worth is at least $169,834—not counting $1,200 worth of blood. The key is to market the body's products intelligently and not reduce them to basic elements like carbon and zinc.

How many muscles does it take to smile? To frown?

One is easier on the face than the other: It takes 17 muscles to smile and 43 to frown.

Why does skin wrinkle when it is exposed at length to water?

The skin on the foot or palm of the hand wrinkles because it expands. The thick, hardened layers of skin swell as water is retained.

How much of your body's heat do you lose by not covering your head in the cold?

Your mother was right. You lose about half to three-fourths of it.

• 11 •

INVENTIONS

◆◆◆◆◆

How did the safety pin originate?
The safety pin as we know it today was not produced until 1849, when American inventor Walter Hunt patented the first modern design. Precursors were developed in Europe about 3,000 years ago and became the standard device for fastening clothes. In the sixth century B.C., Greek and Roman women used a *fibula*, a pin with a coiled middle.

When was the chair developed?
It dates from the third and sixth dynasties of Egypt (c. 2686–2181 B.C.). These early chairs often had legs shaped like animal limbs.

Who developed the abacus?
Probably invented by the Babylonians, it was refined and used by the Romans, Chinese, Arabs, Europeans,

and Asians as late as the seventeenth century. It is still used, in various forms, in the Middle East and Japan.

How old is the Hula-Hoop?

The practice of gyrating with hoops made of grape-vines originated in ancient Egypt, Greece, and Rome. The name *hula*, however, was not used until the 1700s, when British and American missionaries returned home with tales of island hoop-dancers. The modern plastic Hula-Hoop was developed in the 1950s by Richard P. Knerr and Arthur K. ("Spud") Melvin, owners of the Wham-O Manufacturing Company in California. It retailed for $1.98 when the Hula-Hoop craze hit in 1958.

How was the inch developed?

What we now know as the inch (from Latin *uncia*, or "12th part") was defined as ¹/₁₂ foot by the Romans. It was roughly a thumb's breadth, while a foot was roughly the length of a human foot. The Romans introduced the inch to Britain, where it was incorporated into the English system of weights and measures. The English made their own contribution to inch lore: In 1305, King Edward I decreed that an inch should be the measure of three dried barleycorns.

How did the piggy bank get its name?

In the Middle Ages, people stored money in a "pygg jar," made of a clay called *pygg*. By the eighteenth century in England, the name and shape of the receptacle had evolved to "pig bank"—and from there to piggy bank.

When were eyeglasses first worn in Europe?

They first appeared in Italy in the fourteenth century, supposedly introduced by Alessandro di Spina of Florence. Eyeglasses also appeared in China about this time; it is not clear who got the idea first.

Who invented the toothbrush?

The first brush with bristles was developed in China in 1498. Bristles were taken from hogs at first, and later from horses and even badgers. Not until 1938 were nylon bristles—more sanitary and less dangerous—developed by Du Pont.

When did pockets come into fashion?

Not until the end of the sixteenth century. Before that time, men carried their keys and money in pieces of cloth attached to their clothing. The first pocket was an open-side seam in which men placed their pouch of personal items. Eventually the pocket became a permanent part of the trousers. Hip and patch pockets were introduced later.

Where was the first elevator?

The first elevator, called the Flying Chair, was erected in King Louis XV's private apartments in the Palace of Versailles in 1743. It gave him ready access to his mistress, Madame de Châteauroux, on the floor above. The Flying Chair was operated by weights.

Who invented shrapnel?

Henry Shrapnel of England (1761–1842), an artillery officer, invented the so-called shrapnel—a round projectile filled with bullets and equipped with an explosive charge to scatter the shot. In later versions, fragments of the shell casing itself were found to be more deadly than the enclosed bullets. *Shrapnel* today refers to those fragments.

Who invented the rubber band?

Stephen Perry, of the rubber manufacturing firm of Messrs. Perry & Co., patented his design for vulcanized rubber bands on March 17, 1845. Then, as now, the bands were designed to secure "papers, letters, etc."

What was the first manmade plastic?

Called celluloid, it was invented in 1869 by American John Wesley Hyatt. This cellulose nitrate and camphor mixture, though flammable, was strong and pliable enough for use in a variety of common household items. Eventually it was replaced by less flammable synthetic polymers.

How did aspirin get its name?

The *a* came from the first letter of the product's scientific name, acetylsalicylic acid. The *spir* came from *Spiraea ulmaria*, the meadowsweet plant, which was the original source of the compound. The *in* was a common suffix for medications in the late nineteenth century, when aspirin was first marketed.

What was the first chewing gum?

It was the flavorless Adams New York Chewing Gum—Snapping and Stretching, developed by New York inventor Thomas Adams and introduced in 1871. Flavored gum followed in 1875, and bubble gum a decade after that.

What is chamois?

This soft, warm leather is the skin of the Alpine animal of the same name. More often, however, it is specially treated sheepskin.

Who introduced assembly-line production?

It was not Henry Ford. Ransom E. Olds, father of the Oldsmobile, introduced the assembly-line technique to the United States in 1901. In doing so, he increased automobile production from 425 vehicles in 1901 to over 2,500 in 1902. Ford contributed modifications, including the conveyor belt system, which reduced the time it took to build a Model T from $1\frac{1}{2}$ days to 90 minutes.

Who invented the brassiere?

New York socialite Mary Phelps Jacobs patented the first brassiere in 1914. She had devised it for her own use as an alternative to the corset, which showed under her sheer gown. The first bra was made from ribbon and handkerchiefs.

Who invented the air conditioner?

New Yorker Willis Carrier became interested in ventilation systems while he was still an engineering student at Cornell at the turn of the century. Shortly after his graduation, he developed his first air-cooling system for a Brooklyn printer and lithographer. The first air-conditioned movie house opened in Chicago in 1919. By the end of the 1920s, many stores and offices were air-conditioned too.

How does a fan cool a room?

Unlike an air conditioner, it does not cool the air. It actually increases the air temperature because of the heat released by the motor. What makes the room seem cooler is increased air circulation over the skin, which speeds evaporation of moisture.

What was the first instant coffee?

Nescafé, developed by the Nestlé Company and introduced in Switzerland in 1938. It had taken eight years to develop.

When was color television invented?

Scottish engineer John Baird built a working color television in 1928. But it was Hungarian-American inventor Peter Carl Goldmark who, in 1940, developed the first color-television system to be used commercially. Goldmark is also remembered for inventing the 33⅓ RPM long-playing record in 1948.

Who built the first modern computer?

In 1942, the theoretical physicist John V. Atanasoff and his assistant Clifford Berry built the first computer that successfully used vacuum tubes to do mathematical calculations. The machine was called the Atanasoff Berry Computer, or ABC.

• 12 •

LIBRARY OMNIBUS

◆◆◆◆◆

Is chop suey an authentic Chinese dish?

It is an authentic Chinese-*American* dish, created either by a dishwasher in San Francisco around 1860 or by Chinese restaurant owners in Brooklyn in the early 1900s. As befits its origin, *chop* is an English word; *suey* is derived from the Chinese *sui*, meaning "bits."

What is the world's deadliest mushroom?

It is *Amanita phalloides*, the death cap or death cup. Eating this mushroom, which contains five different poisons, causes diarrhea and vomiting within 6 to 12 hours. This is followed by damage to the liver, kidneys, and central nervous system—and, in the majority of cases, coma and death.

Traffic reporters often report "rubbernecking delays" around congested areas. Who are the rubber-neckers and why do they cause delays?

The reporters' term refers to delays caused by overly curious drivers—those who crane their "rubber necks" to see a wreck. The phrase first appeared in print in 1896.

What is the origin of the sentence pounded out by new typists, "Now is the time for all good men to come to the aid of the party"?

Never a political slogan, it was created as a typewriter exercise in 1867 by Charles E. Willer, a Milwaukee court reporter. The sentence was designed to use most of the keys on the typewriter, which had recently been invented by Willer's friend Christopher Latham Sholes.

Can caffeine be lethal?

A moderate dose, such as that in a cup of coffee or in a soft drink, is not harmful unless you are allergic to caffeine or suffer from certain conditions, such as a peptic ulcer. However, large doses can be lethal. Ten grams, or 100 cups of coffee over four hours, can kill the average human.

How did Chicago get its name?

In 1696 a Jesuit, Father Pinet, established a mission for Indians called the Mission of the Guardian Angel. It was set along a stream the Indians had named

Checagon, a word meaning anything big, strong, or powerful. Since the river at that point was sluggish, it is thought that *checagon* actually referred to the wild garlic along the riverbanks.

Who supplies the money for the Nobel Peace Prize?

Alfred Nobel, who made his fortune in the Baker oil fields of Russia and through the sale of dynamite and other explosives, bequeathed $9.2 million for the prize at his death in 1896. Some say his concern over increasing mankind's ability to kill one another led him to endow a peace prize. Today, Nobel Prizes are also awarded in the areas of physics, chemistry, physiology or medicine, and literature.

What was the first supermarket?

Two self-service stores—precursors to supermarkets— opened in California in 1912: the Alpha Beta Food Market in Pomona and Ward's Grocetaria in Ocean Park. The Piggly-Wiggly stores, which opened in 1916 in Memphis, Tennessee, had self-service and checkout counters but did not call themselves supermarkets. The word *supermarket* was not part of a store name until 1933, when the Albers Super Markets opened.

Why is aces and eights the "dead man's hand"?

It was the hand held by Deputy U.S. Marshal James Butler ("Wild Bill") Hickok when he was killed. On August 2, 1876, in a saloon in Deadwood Gulch, Dakota Territory, Hickok was shot in the cheek by fellow poker player Jack McCall. McCall later said he had killed Hickok for shooting his brother.

What causes the most household accidents?

The Consumer Product Safety Commission reports that the five most dangerous sources are: stairs, glass doors, cutlery, glass bottles and jars, and home power tools.

Why are manholes round?

They are round so that their covers cannot be dropped *through* the manhole itself. Squares, rectangles, ovals, and other shapes could be so positioned that they would slip into the manhole. The circular manhole cover rests on a lip that is smaller than the cover. Thus, the size and shape keep the manhole cover from falling into the hole.

How many minks does it take to produce the average mink coat?

It takes 35 to 65. The numbers for other types of fur coats are:

Beaver. 15
Fox. 15 to 25
Ermine. 150
Chinchilla. 60 to 100

What is the difference between *cathartics* and *catharsis*?

A *cathartic* is a medicine that stimulates movement of the bowels. Aristotle, in his *Poetics*, used the medical term *catharsis* (in Greek, literally "purgation" or "purification") as a metaphor for the way a stage tragedy "cleans out" the emotions of a spectator by arousing terror and pity.

How long is a fortnight?

Fourteen days.

What does the *ZIP* in *ZIP code* stand for?

The code was named for the national Zoning Improvement Plan.

What is the most drastic change in temperature on record?

The call is close. Over the course of 12 hours in Granville, North Dakota, on February 21, 1918, the temperature rose 83 degrees. It went from −33 degrees Fahrenheit in the early morning to 50 degrees near the end of the afternoon. But in Fairfield, Montana, over the course of 12 hours on December 24, 1924, the temperature dropped 84 degrees. It was 63 degrees Fahrenheit at noon, falling to −21 degrees by midnight.

What are the highest and lowest temperatures ever recorded?

The highest was 136.4 degrees Fahrenheit at El Azizia, Libya, on September 13, 1922. The lowest was −129 degrees Fahrenheit at Vostok, Antarctica, on July 21, 1983.

When did the first showboat open? When did the last showboat close?

The first showboat was William Chapman's *Floating Theatre*, built at Pittsburgh in 1831. It traveled the system of waterways dominated by the Mississippi and Ohio rivers, bringing entertainment to America's river frontier. Once the river frontier closed and other entertainments beckoned, showboats declined. The last authentic showboat in operation was the *Golden Rod* in 1943.

When did casinos become legal in Atlantic City?

Las Vegas-style casinos were approved by New Jersey voters on Tuesday, November 2, 1976.

How much does a 1-carat diamond weigh?

It weighs 200 milligrams, or 3.086 grains troy. The measurement originally represented the weight of a seed of the carob tree.

Has anyone ever been hit by a meteorite?

At least two people. In September 1954, Mrs. Hewlett Hodges of Sylacauga, Alabama, was hit by a meteorite as she napped in her living room. The rock from space weighed about 10 pounds. In the late 1930s, a Japanese girl was also hit by a small meteorite.

Why is an hour divided into 60 minutes? Why not 10 or 100 minutes?

Because it is based on the sexagesimal system of notation—a system based on the number 60 that predates the decimal system. It was developed about 2400 B.C. by the Sumerians. Since ancient times, the sexagesimal system has been used to divide circles into 360 degrees (60 × 6), each degree into 60 minutes, each minute into 60 seconds. Because clocks have round faces, it seemed sensible to apply the system to the measurement of time.

Is an airplane's black box actually black?

No, it is orange. Inside the box, a stainless-steel tape contains information on the airspeed, altitude, and vertical acceleration. A second orange box contains a tape of the last half-hour of conversation in the cockpit.

What does *Ouija* in *Ouija board* mean?

The board, thought to reveal unconscious thoughts and emotions, is named for the French and German words for yes—*oui* and *ja*.

Where do Pygmies live?

The name Pygmy is used by anthropologists to describe any human group whose males are less than 4 feet, 11 inches in average height. The best-known Pygmy groups are those of tropical Africa, but they also include some of the Bushmen of the Kalahari Desert and the Asian Pygmies known as the Negritos.

Who insures the FDIC?

The Federal Deposit Insurance Corporation—created in 1933 to protect against bank failure by insuring deposits in eligible banks—is entitled to borrow up to $3 billion from the U.S. Treasury. The FDIC has not yet had to use that privilege.

On the $1 bill, what do the words *Annuit Coeptis* mean?

The motto above the eye on the dollar bill means, "He [God] Favored Our Undertakings." The eye represents the all-seeing deity. The pyramid symbolizes strength; it is unfinished to suggest the work ahead.

What does the symbol Ⓤ (a circled *U*) on kosher food represent?

The approval of the Union of Orthodox Jewish Congregations of America.

How many women are quoted in *Bartlett's Familiar Quotations?*

Of the 2,200 persons quoted in the current edition, only 164 are women. This is an astronomical increase over the number quoted in the 1855 first edition—four.

What language contains the most words?

English is the wordiest language, with approximately 455,000 active words and 700,000 dead words.

Why is twenty-one considered the age of legal adulthood?

The practice grew out of British common law. Before the Norman invasion, thirteen or fourteen was considered the age of adulthood, at least among the nobility. But during battles, it was observed that thirteen- and fourteen-year-old nobles were not large or strong enough to carry the heavy armor and lance used in fighting. The age was changed to nineteen and then raised to twenty-one, because nineteen-year-olds who inherited estates did not gain their property until two years later, owing to the lengthy legal processes involved.

When was cigarette advertising banned on television and radio?

It was prohibited as of January 2, 1971.

In nuclear weapons terminology, what is the difference between *first strike* and *first use*?

A *first strike* is a massive initial attack intended to destroy all or most of a nation's strategic nuclear weapons and cripple its ability to retaliate. *First use* is the initial employment of nuclear weapons in response to a conventional attack.

What do the colors of the black liberation flag stand for?

Red stands for the blood of the dead. Black represents pride in the color of the skin. Green is for the promise of a new and better life in Africa.

How are U.S. highways numbered?

Odd-numbered highways move north and south, while those with even numbers move east and west. Highways with one- or two-digit numbers are through routes, often long ones used for distance driving.

Three-digit routes that begin with an even number are usually beltways around a city. Three-digit routes that begin with an odd number are spur routes in a city or town.

Is the moon ever actually blue?

The moon does occasionally appear blue because of dust conditions in the atmosphere. The most famous widely observed blue moon of recent times occurred on September 26, 1950, owing to dust raised by Canadian forest fires.

Who invented the peace symbol?

It was created in 1958 as a nuclear disarmament symbol by the Direct Action Committee, and it was first shown that year at peace marches in England. The forked symbol is actually a composite of the semaphore signals *N* and *D*, representing nuclear disarmament.

What is the world's best-selling cookie?

Not surprisingly, it is the unassuming Oreo, made by Nabisco Brands. The first Oreo was sold in Hoboken, New Jersey, in 1912. Now, over 6 billion are sold each year, which means that $1 of every American's $10 in grocery money goes to the cookie.

How deep is an ocean abyss?

The abyssal zone begins at a depth of 6,600 feet and runs to 19,800 feet. It covers 83 percent of the area of oceans and seas. Water temperature in the abyssal zone is about 39 degrees Fahrenheit.

What is the origin of the term *witch hazel*?

The term *witch hazel* is the common name for the *Hamamelis* plant. The *witch* of the plant's name comes from *wice*, an Anglo-Saxon word for a plant with flexible branches. It is unclear who first used the leaves and bark of witch hazel in toiletries and tonics. Some believe it was the Anglo-Saxons; others think the American Indians first explained its medicinal uses to the Pilgrims.

How does one go about joining the French Foreign Legion?

A first step would be to write to them. The address is: Légion Etrangère, Quartier Vienot, 13400 Aubagne, France.

· 13 ·

LITERATURE

♦♦♦♦♦

What is the earliest use of flashback in Western literature?

In Homer's *Odyssey*, most of Odysseus's adventures are recounted in a flashback set within a larger narrative frame. Odysseus tells his story at the court of the Phaeacians.

How many plays did Aeschylus write?

The "father of Greek tragedy" (525–456 B.C.) wrote some 90 plays, but only 7 have survived. They are:

The Suppliants
The Persians
Seven Against Thebes
Prometheus Bound
Agamemnon
The Libation Bearers
The Furies

In Greek tragedies, what is the difference between *hamartia* and *hubris*?

Hamartia is the fatal flaw that brings a good character to ruin. *Hubris* is pride, the classic example of *hamartia*.

What is the difference between *pathos* and *bathos*?

In a work of art, *pathos* is the quality that evokes sympathy or sorrow; *bathos* evokes only laughter and disgust in its failed attempt to create a grand or pathetic effect.

Was Sinbad the Sailor an Arabian?

He was an Iraqi—a merchant shipwrecked after setting sail from Basra, now Iraq. The story of his seven voyages is told in *The Thousand and One Nights*.

When was *The Tale of Genji* written?

Considered the oldest full novel in the world, it was written in Japan toward the start of the eleventh century.

Who was the Beatrice that Dante wrote about in the *Divine Comedy*?

Probably Beatrice Portinari, daughter of a noble Florentine family and wife of Simone de' Bardi. She died at the age of twenty-four on June 8, 1290, more than two decades before the *Divine Comedy* was completed. Dante fell in love with her when they were both children and dedicated most of his poetry to her.

What is the deepest circle of Hell in Dante's *Inferno*?

It is the Ninth Circle, where betrayers of their family or country are frozen in ice. There, in the center of the earth, a three-headed Lucifer eats at Judas Iscariot and at Cassius and Brutus, betrayers of Julius Caesar.

How many *Canterbury Tales* are there?

There are 24. In the order accepted in standard texts, they are:

Knight's Tale	Physician's Tale
Miller's Tale	Pardoner's Tale
Reeve's Tale	Shipman's Tale
Cook's Tale	Prioress's Tale
Man of Law's Tale	Tale of Sir Thopas
Wife of Bath's Tale	Tale of Melibee
Friar's Tale	Monk's Tale
Summoner's Tale	Nun's Priest's Tale
Clerk's Tale	Second Nun's Tale
Merchant's Tale	Canon's Yeoman's Tale
Squire's Tale	Manciple's Tale
Franklin's Tale	Parson's Tale

Where are Chaucer's pilgrims heading in *The Canterbury Tales*?

They are going to Canterbury Cathedral to visit the shrine of Thomas à Becket, former archbishop of Canterbury. Becket had been assassinated in the cathedral in 1170, following a political disagreement with King Henry II. Pilgrimage to the shrine was a popular journey at the time the *Tales* were written (c. 1387–1400).

In what Shakespeare play does a character "Exit, pursued by a bear"?

In *The Winter's Tale*, Act III, Scene 3. Antigonus, a lord of Sicilia, runs for his life after hearing "A savage clamor!" He doesn't make it; his death is reported later in the scene.

How many sonnets did Shakespeare write?

Shakespeare's *Sonnets* (1609) contains 154 sonnets. The poems fall into two main groups: Numbers 1 to 126 are addressed to a young male friend; numbers 127 to 152 are addressed to a mysterious "dark lady." Sonnets 153 and 154, adaptations of a Greek epigram, don't fit into either of the two categories.

What year is described in Daniel Defoe's *Journal of the Plague Year*?

The book describes the epidemic of bubonic plague that ravaged England in 1665. Defoe's fictionalized account was published in 1722. Defoe himself was only five years old when the plague hit London.

Who were the enemies of the Lilliputians in Swift's *Gulliver's Travels*?

The people of Blefuscu, an island northeast of Lilliput. The people there were as tiny and mean-spirited as the Lilliputians. Swift meant Blefuscu to represent France, while Lilliput represented England.

Where did the character Mrs. Malaprop appear?

In Richard Brinsley Sheridan's 1775 play *The Rivals*. She had a habit of misusing words in sentences like "I would by no means wish a daughter of mine to be a progeny of learning." The character gave rise to the term *malapropism*.

Where was Xanadu?

The Mongol emperor Kublai Khan (1215–1294) had a residence in K'ai-p'ing in southeastern Mongolia. Also known as Shang-Tu, this became Xanadu, the site of the emperor's pleasure garden in Samuel Taylor Coleridge's unfinished poem "Kubla Khan" (1797).

Is anyone specific referred to in the lines " 'Tis better to have loved and lost / Than never to have loved at all"?

These lines from Section 27, Stanza 4 of Alfred, Lord Tennyson's poem *In Memoriam* lament the loss of Tennyson's close friend Arthur Hallam, who died at twenty-two.

Who wrote "Candy is dandy / But liquor is quicker"?

Ogden Nash wrote the ditty in 1931. In 1968, he updated it:

> Candy is dandy
> But liquor is quicker.
> Pot is not.

What were the real names behind these famous pen names?

Boz. Charles Dickens
George Eliot. Mary Ann Evans
George Orwell. Eric Arthur Blair

Ellery Queen. Frederic Dannay and Manfred B. Lee
Stendhal. Marie-Henri Beyle
Saki. Hector Hugh Munro
Voltaire. François-Marie Arouet
Maksim Gorki. Aleksei Maksimovich Peshkov

What was the first American novel?

In 1789, *The Power of Sympathy* by William Hill Brown was published. This first American novel, written by the son of a Boston clockmaker, concerned seduction, incest, rape, and suicide.

Who wrote "Mary Had a Little Lamb"?

One of the earliest and most influential American magazine editors, Sarah Josepha Hale—in 1830. In addition to founding the first national women's magazine, *Godey's Ladies' Magazine*, and successfully campaigning to make Thanksgiving a national holiday, she was inspired to write the rhyme by an actual case of a child's being followed to school by a pet lamb.

What was Hiawatha's tribe?

The hero of Longfellow's *Song of Hiawatha* (1855) belonged to the Mohawk tribe, one of the Five Nations of the Iroquois.

Did the Brontë sisters publish their novels under their own names?

No, they used male pseudonyms: Charlotte was Currer Bell; Emily was Ellis Bell; and Anne was Acton Bell.

What was Pip's real name in *Great Expectations*?
Philip Pirrip.

Were Lewis Carroll's "Alice" books written for anyone?
They are said to have been written for a friend, Alice Liddell, who, with three other children on an 1862 boating trip, inspired the first of the stories, which Carroll initially called *Alice's Adventures Underground*. The book, with additional tales as well as illustrations, was published in 1865, followed in 1871 by *Through the Looking-Glass and What Alice Found There*.

How many Brothers Karamazov are there?
In Dostoyevsky's 1880 novel, Fyodor Pavlovich Karamazov has four sons: Dmitri, Ivan, Alyosha, and Smerdyakov, a bastard. Dmitri is the son accused of killing his father.

Was there a real Dr. Jekyll and Mr. Hyde?
No, but there was a Scottish cabinetmaker named William Brodie who inspired Robert Louis Stevenson's story. Brodie, a respected businessman by day, wore a mask and led a gang of robbers by night. Born in 1741, Brodie was hanged in 1788. The story interested Stevenson and inspired *The Strange Case of Dr. Jekyll and Mr. Hyde* (1886).

Whatever became of Sherlock Holmes's rival Moriarty?
Professor James Moriarty, "the Napoleon of Crime," was killed when he and Holmes, locked in combat, fell

over the edge of the Reichenbach Falls in Switzerland. Amazingly, Holmes survived.

What is the origin of the journalistic term *muckraker*?

Shortly after the turn of the century, President Theodore Roosevelt said that the writers of exposés who flourished at the time reminded him of John Bunyan's Man with the Muckrake, who, when offered a heavenly crown, "would neither look up nor regard the crown he was offered, but continued to rake to himself the filth of the floor."

How did the kingdom of Oz get its name?

Although some biographers believe the story of Oz's naming to be as fanciful as the tales themselves, author L. Frank Baum claimed that he was inspired by a file cabinet marked O–Z. Other suggested derivations include: a variation on Uz, Job's house; a variation of children's *oh*'s and *ah*'s; and a variation of Boz, the pseudonym for Charles Dickens, one of Baum's favorite authors.

Where in Santayana's works does the line "Those who cannot remember the past are condemned to repeat it" appear?

It appears in the first volume of *The Life of Reason: Reason in Common Sense* (1905–1906). The philosopher George Santayana (1863–1952) did *not* say any of the common variations: "Those who do not learn from history ... Those who cannot learn ... Those who will not learn ..."

What is the difference between a bildungsroman and a roman à clef?

A bildungsroman (in German, it means "education novel") deals with the formation of a young person and includes common coming-of-age stories. James Joyce's *Portrait of the Artist as a Young Man* (1916) is an example. A roman à clef (in French, it means a "novel with a key") contains one or more characters or situations based on real-life models. Theodore Dreiser's *American Tragedy* (1925)—based on a 1906 murder in the Adirondacks—is an example.

What is a doppelgänger?

Derived from the German words *Doppel* (double) and *Gänger* (walker), a doppelgänger is the personification of another side of a character's personality. The apparition often represents a demonic side and may herald oncoming death.

Who was the first woman to win the Pulitzer Prize for fiction?

It was Edith Wharton (1862–1937) in 1921 for *The Age of Innocence*.

Who was the first recipient of the Nobel Prize for literature?

René François Armand Sully Prudhomme of France in 1901.

Who was the first English writer to receive the prize?
Rudyard Kipling in 1907.

The first American?
Sinclair Lewis in 1930.

What was the actual case behind *An American Tragedy*?

The 1925 novel by Theodore Dreiser (1871–1945) was based on the murder of the pregnant Grace Brown by her boyfriend, social climber Chester Gillette, at Big Moose Lake in the Adirondacks in 1906.

Who created Charlie Chan?

Ohio-born writer Earl Derr Biggers invented the portly Honolulu detective. The first book about Chan was *The House Without a Key* (1925).

Who was Dr. Fu Manchu's arch-adversary?

The Chinese master criminal, who appeared in 13 novels by Sax Rohmer beginning in 1913, received his main opposition from Sir Denis Nayland Smith, loosely connected with Scotland Yard. Smith's sidekick was Dr. Petrie.

Who sat at the famous Algonquin Round Table?

The wits who traded barbs at New York's Algonquin Hotel in the 1920s included: Franklin P. Adams, Robert Benchley, Heywood Broun, Frank Case, Edna Ferber, George S. Kaufman, Harpo Marx, Neysa McMein, Dorothy Parker, Harold Ross, Robert E.

Sherwood, and Alexander Woollcott. The Algonquin Hotel still stands. It was recently sold to a group of Japanese investors.

Was Erle Stanley Gardner, the creator of Perry Mason, ever a lawyer?

Yes. Born in 1889, he was admitted to the California bar in 1911 and was known for defending poor Chinese and Mexicans. In the 1940s, he founded the Court of Last Resort—an organization dedicated to helping people unjustly imprisoned.

Was there ever a real Shangri-La?

The setting for James Hilton's 1933 novel *Lost Horizon* supposedly has a real-life counterpart in Hunza, Pakistan. The community, which boasts of having the healthiest people in the world, many over 100 years old, is located at the borders of Pakistan, China, and the Soviet Union.

How many copies of *Gone with the Wind* have been sold?

Margaret Mitchell's 1937 Pulitzer Prize–winner has been translated into 27 languages and has sold over 20 million copies.

What is the book written without using the letter *e*?

It is a 1939 novel called *Gadsby* by Ernest Vincent Wright (1872–1939). The novel runs 267 pages and has about 50,000 words.

Was the author of the James Bond novels ever an agent himself?

Yes. Ian Fleming (1908–1964) began his intelligence work during World War II, when he served as the director of Naval Intelligence in Britain. After D Day, he was placed in charge of an assault unit that became known as Fleming's Private Navy. It obtained German code books and equipment as British troops moved through France.

What won Charles Lindbergh the Pulitzer Prize?

The transatlantic flier and isolationist won the Pulitzer Prize in 1953 for his autobiography, *The Spirit of St. Louis*. The book was made into a movie starring James Stewart in 1957.

How old was Lolita when Humbert Humbert first met her?

She was twelve.

What was the original Catch-22?

In Joseph Heller's 1961 novel of the same name, it is the catch that prevents a U.S. Air Force pilot from asking to be grounded on the basis of insanity. A man "would be crazy to fly more missions and sane if he didn't, but if he was sane, he had to fly them. If he flew them he was crazy and didn't have to; but if he didn't, he was sane and had to."

What was Isaac Asimov's first book?

Written in 1950, when he was thirty, it was *Pebble in the Sky*.

> *How many books has Asimov written?*
> The Russian-born writer has over 400 books to his credit, including science fiction, science nonfiction, mystery, textbooks, and a guide to Shakespeare.

• 14 •

MYTH AND FOLKLORE

◆◆◆◆◆

From which god did the Egyptian pharaohs claim to be descended?

Ra, the sun-god—sometimes represented with the disk of the sun on his head and surrounded by Uraeus, the sacred flame-breathing asp.

How many knights sat at the Round Table?

The Round Table seated 150 knights, with one place left open for the Holy Grail. The table's design was conceived by Merlin to prevent any bickering about who would get places of honor.

Do any animals besides black cats supposedly bring bad fortune?

Yes—hares. Legend has it that witches transform themselves into hares, so crossing a hare's path may mean meeting up with a witch. Further, hares have been believed by some to be melancholy creatures; thus, eating a hare can ruin your day.

How did the rabbit's foot come to be considered a good luck charm?

In Western Europe, people have considered the feet of rabbits lucky since before 600 B.C. Several characteristics of the rabbit may have led to its great popularity: It is born with its eyes open, suggesting innate wisdom; it spends much of its life underground, suggesting a connection to a mysterious netherworld; it is prolific, suggesting wealth and prosperity. Any part of the rabbit was considered lucky, but the foot was especially prized—possibly as a phallic or fertility symbol.

Who were the parents of Apollo and Dionysus?

Both Greek gods were fathered by Zeus, king of the gods. Apollo's mother was the goddess Leto; Dionysus's mother was a mortal named Semele. Apollo was the god of light, healing, music, and archery. Dionysus, a darker figure, was the god of wine and fertility.

Who were Zeus's parents?

They were both Titans, children of Uranus (Sky) and Gaea (Earth). Zeus's mother was Rhea; his father was Cronus. Fearing that one of his sons would overthrow him, Cronus swallowed his five other children, but Rhea rescued Zeus and had him raised in secrecy in a cave. Eventually Zeus tricked Cronus into vomiting up the other children and overthrew the old god.

What is the original use of the word *chaos*?

In Greek mythology, Chaos was the primal void that gave birth to Gaea (Earth), Tartarus (Infernal Regions), Eros (Love), Erebus (Darkness), and Nyx (Night).

Who were the Cyclopes?

They were giants born of Uranus (Sky) and Gaea (Earth). Each of them had the characteristic single eye in the middle of the forehead. The most famous Cyclops, Polyphemus, ate some of Odysseus's crewmen in *The Odyssey*. Others—Brontes, Steropes, and Arges— were famed for having fashioned Zeus's thunderbolts.

Why did Greek sailors like Nereids?

These 50 nymphs of the sea—daughters of the sea-god Nereus—often came to the aid of sailors in trouble.

Who came up with the idea that newborn babies are delivered by the stork?

The ancient Scandinavians appear to be responsible for this legend, which grew out of observations of storks— their nesting in chimneys, their monogamy, and their gentle behavior toward their kin. The myth did not gain worldwide acceptance until the nineteenth century, when Danish writer Hans Christian Andersen popularized it in his fairy tales.

When did the practice of wearing wedding rings become popular? Why is the ring worn on the third finger (not counting the thumb) of the left hand?

Some believe the practice is a vestige of ancient barbarian marriages—when a man would capture a woman and bind her to his house in fetters, now symbolized by a ring. Others think the practice originated in ancient Egypt about 2800 B.C. As the circular ring has no beginning or end, it is the perfect symbol of the eternal bond of marriage.

The custom of wearing the wedding ring on the third finger of the left hand began with the Greeks in the third century B.C. Greek physicians believed that this finger contained a "vein of love" that ran directly to the heart.

Why is black the color of mourning in the Western world?

In ancient times, it was believed that the spirits of the dead could repossess the bodies of the living. So, to disguise themselves from evil spirits, mourners painted their bodies black. Later societies translated this custom into wearing black clothes and veils.

Was there a Mother Goose?

Yes, according to legend. She was Elizabeth Goose, a New England widow who married Isaac Goose, adopting a family of 10, and later bore 6 children. In 1719, her book of rhymes—*Mother Goose's Melodies for Children*—was said to have been published by her son-in-law. No copy of the book has ever been found. A more likely choice for the originator of Mother Goose is French author Charles Perrault. In 1697, he published *Tales of My Mother Goose*. The character was possibly derived from a character in German folklore, Frau Gosen, or else invented by Perrault himself.

What did the swastika stand for before Hitler appropriated it?

Before it became the Nazi symbol of Aryan superiority, the swastika had several meanings, all positive. In Sanskrit, the word *swastika* means "conducive to well-being." The Aryans of India believed swastikas represented the sun's motion across the sky, a symbol of its goodness and regenerative power. The Greeks and Persians believed it represented prosperity and happiness. Early Christians disguised the cross as a swastika to avoid persecution. North American Indian tribes used a similar symbol as a sign of peace.

Why is spilling salt considered bad luck?

One reason is because salt was once valuable and difficult to obtain. According to an old Norwegian superstition, a person is doomed to shed as many tears as it takes to dissolve the spilled salt. Another reason is the belief that spilled salt refers to the devil. In the German superstition, whoever spills salt engenders enmity: It is thought to be a direct act of the devil. And both the French and the Americans toss salt over the left shoulder to hit the devil in the eye.

What do you get when you kiss the Blarney Stone?

According to legend, the gift of eloquence. To reach the Blarney Stone, go to the southern wall of Blarney Castle in the village of Blarney, County Cork, Ireland. The stone is under the battlements there. Be warned: You have to hang head downward to kiss it.

Who were Sir Galahad's parents?

As presented in Thomas Malory's *Morte d'Arthur*, Sir Galahad was the illegitimate son of Sir Lancelot and Princess Elaine. Also the last descendant of Joseph of Arimathea, he was the purest knight of the Knights of the Round Table.

Who is the Lady of the Lake?

In Malory's *Morte d'Arthur*, she is a supernatural figure who lives in a magical lake. She steals the infant Lancelot and raises him in the lake—hence his name, Lancelot du Lac. She also awards King Arthur the sword Excalibur, which he takes from an arm reaching out of the lake. *The Lady of the Lake* is also a poem by Sir Walter Scott (1771–1832).

What were the labors of Hercules?

Over the course of 12 years' service to Eurystheus, king of Mycenae, Hercules performed the following:

1. Killed the Nemean lion
2. Killed the hydra of Lerna
3. Captured the Erymanthian boar

4. Captured the hind of Artemis
5. Killed the man-eating Stymphalian birds
6. Cleaned the Augean stables
7. Captured the Cretan bull
8. Captured the horses of Diomedes
9. Captured the girdle of Hippolyte
10. Captured the cattle of the monster Geryon
11. Captured Cerberus, the three-headed dog
12. Stole the golden apples of the Hesperides

Who were the Muses?

They were the nine daughters of Zeus and Mnemosyne. Originally there were only three, associated with memory; their number was expanded to nine to represent each of the individual arts. They are:

1. Calliope, muse of epic poetry
2. Clio, muse of heroic poetry or history
3. Erato, muse of love poetry
4. Euterpe, muse of music
5. Melpomene, muse of tragedy
6. Polyhymnia, muse of sacred poetry and hymns
7. Terpsichore, muse of choral song and dance
8. Thalia, muse of comedy
9. Urania, muse of astronomy

Why was Sisyphus punished?

It is well known that Sisyphus was punished in Hades by having to roll a stone forever up a hill, only to have it roll back down. It is less well known that he was given this sentence as punishment for cheating death. Sisyphus, a king of Corinth, was a master trickster who planned the ultimate prank. He told his wife that when he died she was to dishonor his body. Upon his death, she did so. He used the affront as an excuse to come back to life, supposedly for the purpose of punishing his wife. When he returned home to her, he stayed—and lived a second long, full life.

How was Tantalus tantalized?

The Phrygian king Tantalus, who committed an abomination when he cut up his son Pelops and served him for dinner to the gods, was punished in Hades by unending thirst and hunger. Water slipped away from him whenever he tried to drink it; fruit trees were forever out of reach. This story is the source of the modern word *tantalize*.

Who is Nike?

In Greek mythology, Nike was the goddess of victory. She was the daughter of the giant Pallas and the river Styx. In Rome, Nike was called Victoria.

What was the Greek god Priapus known for?

Priapus, a god of animal and plant fertility, was known for his enormous phallus. He was usually described as the son of Dionysus and Aphrodite, though sometimes his mother was said to have been a local nymph. To sophisticated city-dwellers, Priapus often became the subject of racy humor, but rural people adopted him as the god of gardens; some even used his statue as a scarecrow.

Who were the three Graces?

Daughters of Zeus, they were Greek goddesses of fertility, later associated with beauty and love—Aglaia (Brightness), Euphrosyne (Joyfulness), and Thalia (Bloom). Their collective name, Graces (they were also known as Chorites), referred to the gracious or pleasing appearance of fertile gardens and fields.

Is there a Vanity Fair?

The fair exists in literature, created by John Bunyan in *The Pilgrim's Progress* (Part I, 1678; Part II, 1684). Established in the town of Vanity by Beelzebub, Apollyon, and Legion, it lasts all year and sells all manner of earthly treasures and enjoyments.

What was the philosophers' stone?

In medieval times, it was the substance that alchemists claimed would turn base metals into gold. The great search for the stone laid the groundwork for the development of the science of chemistry.

Where was Prester John's empire?

The legendary Christian ruler was believed to have reigned in Asia beyond Persia and Armenia, under the humble title Presbyter or Prester—that is, priest. European Christians hoped Prester John would help them drive the Muslims out of the Holy Land. Explorers like

Marco Polo went looking for him; at least one forged letter was sent to Europe in Prester John's name. In the fourteenth century, legend had it that he ruled in Ethiopia, not Asia. But Prester John was never found.

Why do people cross their fingers for good luck?
The practice may have evolved from the sign of the cross, which was believed to ward off evil.

What do pixies do?
These mischievous sprites of English folklore like to play pranks on people. They are most famous for leading people astray. Hence, anyone lost on a familiar road, bewildered, or confused came to be called "pixie-led" or "pixilated."

What does "The Grateful Dead" mean to a folklorist?
It does not mean a rock group. It is a folktale in which a young man buries a corpse at great personal risk, then obtains a bride with the help of the grateful deceased. A version of the tale appears in the apocryphal Old Testament book of Tobit.

On how many mattresses did the princess in "The Princess and the Pea" sleep?
She slept on 20 mattresses and 20 eiderdowns (fluffy featherbeds), between 2 of which was placed a single pea.

Who was Tammuz and what does he have to do with Adonis?

The Greek Adonis, the Babylonian Tammuz, the Sumerian Dumuzi, and the Egyptian Osiris are all forms of the same god. After being carried off to the underworld, Tammuz, god of crops and vegetation, was rescued by his lover Ishtar. All life on earth withered between his dying (in winter) and his rising (in spring).

What does Tammuz mean to Jews?

In the Jewish calendar, it is the name of the month that falls during June and July.

Who was Ishtar?

She was the great mother goddess of the Babylonians and Assyrians. Her concerns included fertility, healing, sexuality, and lust.

Who was Quetzalcoatl?

He was the Aztec god of the atmosphere and of civilizing influences. Besides ruling the wind and sun, he invented agriculture, the calendar, and many arts and crafts. Sometimes represented as a feathered serpent, sometimes as a bearded man, he was also identified as a priest-king who had sailed away, promising to return.

What is Ragnarok in Norse mythology?

It is the day of doom and corresponds to Götterdämmerung, the Teutonic Twilight of the Gods. On Ragnarok, a battle between good and evil results in the world's being consumed by fire. Later, a new world, new humans, and new gods spring up around the core of a few survivors.

Which is the female half of yin and yang?

Yin is female, dark, negative, earthly. Yang is male, bright, positive, heavenly. In Chinese mythology, both are ethers born in the division of the original cell of chaos, Ch'i.

When was the last time you could have taken part in a bacchanalia?

The last legal one was in the second century B.C.— before the Roman senate banned this festival honoring Bacchus, the Roman god of wine. Originally a religious rite celebrated only by women, it eventually included men and became an excuse for drunken orgies.

◆ 15 ◆

NEW YORK CITY
HISTORY

◆◆◆◆◆

What are the dimensions of Manhattan Island?
Manhattan is 13.4 miles long, 2.3 miles across at its widest point, and 22.5 square miles in area.

Who first sighted the land that became New York City?
Giovanni da Verrazano, an Italian explorer, first sighted Manhattan in 1524, but English explorer Henry Hudson, who sailed into what is now known as the Hudson River in 1609, is credited as the island's discoverer.

How did New York's Tammany Hall get its name?
The headquarters for the Democratic party organization was once a social club named for a seventeenth-

146

century Delaware Indian chief. After the Revolution, Aaron Burr transformed it into a political machine, using it to strengthen the 1800 presidential campaign of Thomas Jefferson. Its power grew throughout the nineteenth century and Tammany Hall became the nexus of all political activity in the city.

When did the New York Stock Exchange open?

The New York Stock and Exchange Board was formally organized in 1817, and the name New York Stock Exchange was adopted in 1863. Since 1953, membership in the exchange has been limited to 1,366. Since 1868, new members have purchased seats (with exchange approval) from existing members.

When did Central Park open to the public?

October 1858.

When was Tavern-on-the-Green built?

Tavern-on-the-Green in Central Park was built in 1870—not as a restaurant but to house sheep and their shepherd and his family. In 1934, the sheep were moved to Prospect Park in Brooklyn and the building was converted to a restaurant. Glass pavilions were added to the original brick structure from 1975 to 1976.

How many Madison Square Gardens have there been?

Four—but only the first two were on Madison Square, at Madison Avenue and East Twenty-sixth Street. The first arena, originally a railroad depot, was given the name Madison Square Garden in 1879. The second was designed by Stanford White and built in 1890. The third, located between Forty-ninth and Fiftieth Streets on Eighth Avenue, rose in 1925. The fourth was built in 1968 and extends from West Thirty-first to West Thirty-third Streets between Seventh and Eighth Avenues.

What was New York's Ladies' Mile?

In the late 1800s, it was Manhattan's high-class shopping district. This equivalent of Fifth Avenue or Fifty-seventh Street ran from Eighth Street to Twenty-third Street, bound on the east by Broadway and on the west by Sixth Avenue—areas now parts of the more residential neighborhoods of Greenwich Village and Chelsea.

When did Harlem become a black neighborhood?

In the nineteenth century, the district known as Harlem in northern Manhattan was a fashionable white residential district, a favorite site for summer homes. Apartment buildings rose in the boom of the 1880s. After the panic of 1893, however, many buildings became vacant, and property owners began renting to blacks. By World War I, much of Harlem had become black. But as late as the 1930s, blacks were kept out of some parts of the neighborhood.

What was the first electric sign in New York?

Erected in June 1892 on a nine-story building near Broadway and Twenty-third Street, it measured 60 by 68 feet and read:

Buy Homes On
Long Island
Swept By Ocean Breezes
Manhattan Beach
Oriental Hotel
Manhattan Hotel
Gilmore's Band
Brock's Fireworks

Why are there only 400 members of New York society's so-called Four Hundred?

New York socialite Samuel Ward McAllister created the term in 1892, when he planned a party to be held in Mrs. William Astor's ballroom. Since the ballroom held only 400 people, McAllister limited the invitations to those he decided were the inner elite of New York society.

What gave Times Square its name?

It was named for the 1903 building that was headquarters for the *New York Times*. The building, located at the intersection of Seventh Avenue, Forty-second Street, and Broadway, transmitted news by the band of electric lights that ran across the top of the building. *New York Newsday* now occupies the spot and still flashes headlines as its predecessor did.

How many women died in the Triangle Waist Company fire in New York City?

At least 146 women, mainly young immigrants, died in the sweatshop fire that occurred on April 20, 1911.

The sprinkler system was inadequate, the 500 female workers stood back-to-back on the crowded work floors, and the fire doors were kept locked to prevent theft. The company owners were later acquitted of manslaughter charges.

What used to stand at the site of the Empire State Building?

Until 1929, the Waldorf-Astoria stood at the southwest corner of Thirty-fourth Street and Fifth Avenue. On October 1 of that year, demolition of the famous hotel began, and on May 1, 1931, the Empire State Building opened on the space. In the same year, the Waldorf reopened at its current address between Forty-ninth and Fiftieth Streets on Park Avenue.

What were the first and last regular showings of movies in Radio City Music Hall?

Its first movie was *The Bitter Tea of General Yen*, directed by Frank Capra and starring Barbara Stanwyck and Nils Asther. It opened in January 1934. The final movie was *The Promise*, directed by Gilbert Cates and starring Kathleen Quinlan and Stephen Collins. The final showing was on April 25, 1979. Since that time, the theater has presented musical shows and other special engagements.

What was the location of the Hotel Pennsylvania, inspiration for Glenn Miller's song "Pennsylvania 6-5000"?

The hotel was located at Seventh Avenue and Thirty-third Street in Manhattan. It was built in 1918. The phone number Pennsylvania 6-5000 was that of the hotel's Club Rouge, where Miller and his band often appeared. The hotel is now the New York Penta Hotel.

For how long did New York City have a Miss Subways?

The program, run by the New York Subway Advertising Company, started in May 1941 and ended in December 1976. Every month a Miss Subways—a woman over 17, not an actress or a model—was chosen. She was featured on signs and was given a $50 sterling silver charm with dangling subway tokens. The first Miss Subways was future movie actress Mona Freeman; the last was Heide Hafner.

When was Sixth Avenue renamed Avenue of the Americas?

On October 2, 1945, when Mayor Fiorello La Guardia (1882–1947) signed a bill officially changing the name to honor all the countries of the two continents.

Where was Needle Park?

The infamous hangout for addicts and dealers in the 1960s and 1970s was Verdi Square Park, named for the Italian composer, which occupies a triangular area between Seventy-second and Seventy-third Streets at Broadway and Amsterdam Avenue.

When was the last smoke ring blown from a cigarette billboard in Times Square?

The final smoking sign, which had advertised Winston cigarettes for five years, stopped blowing rings September 13, 1977. Like its predecessors for much of the twentieth century, it blew about 1,000 rings a day; a steam-producing box, located behind the head of the man in the sign, created the rings. The Winston sign had replaced the Camel sign, which operated from 1941 to 1966 on Broadway between Forty-third and Forty-fourth Streets.

Can people still meet under the Biltmore clock in New York City?

Yes, but the clock that once hung over the entrance to the lavish Palm Court salon in the famed Biltmore Hotel—between Madison and Vanderbilt Avenues and Forty-third and Forty-fourth Streets—is now part of the 78-story atrium of the Bank of America Plaza at 335 Madison Avenue. The bronze clock is the only visible remnant of the Palm Court, which was demolished in August 1981 when the hotel was converted into a bank building.

What is the highest natural elevation in the New York metropolitan area?

Todt Hill, on Staten Island, at 426 feet. In fact, it is the highest point on the eastern seaboard south of Maine. Cadillac Mountain in Maine is the highest point on the eastern seaboard.

What are the five tallest buildings in New York City?

World Trade Center. 1,350 feet high, 110 stories
Empire State Building. 1,250 feet high, 102 stories

(with the 164-foot television tower included, it is
1,414 feet high)
Chrysler Building. 1,046 feet high, 77 stories
AT&T Building. 950 feet high, 67 stories
40 Wall Tower. 927 feet high, 71 stories

What is the speed limit in New York City?

Thirty miles per hour on the streets, 50 miles per hour
on the highways, except where otherwise noted.

• 16 •

POPULAR CULTURE

•••••

Where does the word *vaudeville* come from?

Originally referring to a type of light, comedic song that originated in Vau-de-Vire in Normandy, France, it came to mean the whole program of songs, dances, comedy, and other acts once popular in theaters across America. Vaudeville was introduced to the United States in 1865 with the opening of the Opera House, a theater in New York City. The greatest vaudeville showplace in the country, the Palace Theatre (also in New York), closed in 1932.

Does the "old soft-shoe" have anything to do with soft shoes?

Soft-shoe was one of two distinct styles of tap dancing developed in the late nineteenth century. Easygoing and smooth, it required soft-soled shoes. In contrast, the fast, energetic buck-and-wing employed wooden-soled shoes. The two styles merged by 1925, with metal taps added to the toes and heels.

What is the most widely sung song in the English-speaking world?

It is "Happy Birthday to You," which was adapted from "Good Morning to You!" by Mildred J. and Patty S. Hill.

Who was the first movie star?

While early American filmmakers refused to reveal the names of their players, fearing the actors would request more money, German filmgoers created celebrities. The first celebrity actress was Henny Porten, who first appeared in the movie *Lohengrin* (1907), directed by Oskar Messter. She was known only as the Messter Girl until 1909, when she played the romantic lead in *Das Liebesglück der Blinden* (*The Love of the Blind Girl*) to such fanfare that Messter was requested to reveal her name to the public. Soon thereafter, Porten asked for a raise.

Who was the first movie reviewer?

Using the pseudonym Spectator, Frank E. Woods began the tradition in the June 1908 issue of the *New York Dramatic Mirror*. Six years later, the *Chicago Tribune* began the first regular publication of movie reviews. The first columnist was Jack Lawson; when he died shortly after the feature's inauguration, Miss Audrie Alspaugh took over. Under the pseudonym Kitty

Kelly, she turned the review into a force the studios had to reckon with.

What was the first cartoon shown in U.S. movie theaters with a regular feature?

In 1909, *Gertie the Dinosaur*, created by *New York Journal* cartoonist Winsor McKay, became the first cartoon shown in movie houses along with a regular feature.

What was the Keystone that gave the Keystone Kops their name?

The Keystone Company was the movie studio formed by Mack Sennett in 1912. The Kops appeared in a number of the studio's more than 1,000 comedy shorts.

What did Fatty Arbuckle do that ruined his career?

In 1921, the 320-pound silent comedy star and former Keystone Kop allegedly caused the death of a young starlet, Virginia Rappe, fiancée of the director of some of Arbuckle's films. At a wild party in San Francisco, Rappe went into convulsions, supposedly the result of a sexual assault by Arbuckle. She died a few days later. Arbuckle stood trial for manslaughter; two trials ended in hung juries, the third acquitted him. But the notoriety ended his career. He died forgotten in 1933.

What were the measurements of the perfect Ziegfeld Girl?

For the showgirls who appeared in the *Ziegfeld Follies*, which ran from 1907 into the 1930s, impresario Florenz Ziegfeld insisted on women with the following measurements: bust, 36 inches; waist, 26 inches; and hips, 38 inches. It is estimated that only 3,000 of the 200,000 applicants over the years met these requirements.

What was the first full-scale collaboration between George and Ira Gershwin?

The Broadway musical *Lady Be Good* in 1924. It included the songs "Fascinating Rhythm" and "Oh Lady, Be Good."

What was the greatest number of kisses in a single film?

One hundred twenty-seven in *Don Juan* (1926). Mary Astor and Estelle Taylor received the kisses from John Barrymore.

Where did the actor Stepin Fetchit get his name?

Born Lincoln Theodore Monroe Andrew Perry in 1902, the black actor got his stage name from a racehorse on which he bet and won a large sum of money. The name has since become a term of derision among blacks for someone subservient to whites. Fetchit died in 1985.

When was the Hays Code, which regulated moviemaking, instituted?

The Motion Picture Production Code, devised by the Motion Picture Association of America and nicknamed the Hays Code for the MPAA's first director, Will H.

Hays, was adopted in 1930. The lengthy document, which was written to forestall government censorship of movies, was not dissolved by the MPAA until 1968.

Who was the youngest person to win an Oscar and for what film(s)?

Shirley Temple, aged five, was presented a miniature Oscar statuette "in grateful recognition of her outstanding contributions to screen entertainment during the year 1934" for such films as *Stand Up and Cheer*, *Little Miss Marker*, and *Bright Eyes*.

Who was the youngest actor or actress to win an Oscar in a standard category?

Ten-year-old Tatum O'Neal, in 1973, for Best Supporting Actress in Peter Bogdanovich's *Paper Moon*.

Who first sang "Santa Claus Is Comin' to Town"?

Eddie Cantor sang it on his radio show one week before Thanksgiving 1934. It was written in 1932 by Haven Gillespie and J. Fred Coots.

How did Bugs Bunny get his name?

The character was created in 1936 by a group of artists at Warner Bros., including Chuck Jones and Friz Freleng. The original sketches, however, were submitted by a Warner story man Ben ("Bugs") Hardaway. He marked the drawings "Bugs Bunny." The rest is history.

Who came first, Superman or Batman?

Superman first appeared in Action Comics No. 1, June 1938. Batman first appeared in Detective Comics No. 27, May 1939.

What are Superman's superpowers?

He is virtually invulnerable (with Kryptonite being his major weakness; its rays are fatal to him); he is super-strong, superfast, and supersmart; he can fly; he has heat vision, X-ray vision, telescopic vision, and micro-scopic vision; he has quick-freezing, gale-force breath; he has supersensitive hearing; and he can hold his breath for long periods.

Does Batman have any superpowers?

No. He is, however, the master of every known martial art and an accomplished scientist and detective.

In *The Wizard of Oz*, what is Dorothy's last name?

Gale.

What are the real names of:

Fred Astaire. Frederick Austerlitz
Bing Crosby. Harry Lillis Crosby
Marlene Dietrich. Maria Magdalene von Losch
W. C. Fields. William Claude Dukenfield
Greta Garbo. Greta Gustafsson
Judy Garland. Frances Gumm

Cary Grant. Archibald Alexander Leach
Boris Karloff. William Henry Pratt
John Wayne. Marion Michael Morrison

Who started the craze of eating goldfish?

A Harvard University student named Lothrop With-
ington, Jr., swallowed a 4-inch goldfish on a bet on
March 3, 1939. The event was publicized in the Boston
papers and soon created a new campus fad.

What was the complete lineup in Abbott and Cos-
tello's "Who's on First" comedy routine?

First Base. Who
Second Base. What
Third Base. I Don't Know
Shortstop. I Don't Give a Darn (I Don't Care)
Catcher. Today
Pitcher. Tomorrow
Left Field. Why
Center Field. Because
Right Field. Not mentioned in the routine

How old was Greta Garbo when she retired from
the movie business? What was her last film?

She was thirty-six when she retired, after making *Two-
Faced Woman* in 1941. She never explained why she
retired. She lived on Manhattan's Upper East Side until
her death in April 1990.

What was the first gold record? The first gold album?

Glenn Miller was presented with a gold-covered master of his recording "Chattanooga Choo Choo" on his radio program of February 10, 1942. The record—released in conjunction with the 1941 movie *Sun Valley Serenade*—had climbed past the 1 million mark a few months after its release. The original 1949 Broadway cast recording of *Oklahoma!* became the first long-playing album to sell more than 1 million copies. By 1956, 1.75 million copies had been sold.

Was "As Time Goes By" written for *Casablanca*?

No, the 1931 hit by Herman Hupfeld was first performed by Frances Williams in *Everybody's Welcome*. Rudy Vallee recorded a hit version of the song, but its greatest popularity came from *Casablanca*.

In how many films did Basil Rathbone play Sherlock Holmes?

Fourteen. The first was *The Hound of the Baskervilles* in 1939. The last was *Dressed to Kill* in 1946.

How many road pictures did Hope, Crosby, and Lamour make?

There were seven:

Road to Singapore (1940)
Road to Zanzibar (1941)
Road to Morocco (1942)

Road to Utopia (1946)
Road to Rio (1947)
Road to Bali (1953)
Road to Hong Kong (1962)

Who were the Hollywood Ten?

They were a group of Hollywood writers and artists who were blacklisted after their appearances before the House Un-American Activities Committee (HUAC) in 1947 and 1948. HUAC was set up to investigate "the extent of Communist infiltration in the Hollywood motion picture industry." It cited the following artists for contempt of Congress for refusing to list their political affiliations: screenwriters Alvah Bessie, Lester Cole, Ring Lardner, Jr., John Howard Lawson, Albert Maltz, Samuel Ornitz, and Dalton Trumbo; producer-director Herbert Biberman; director Edward Dmytryk; and producer-writer Adrian Scott. In 1948, the ten were tried in the Federal Court of Washington, D.C., convicted of contempt of Congress, and sentenced to a year in jail and fined $1,000.

Which performer has appeared in the greatest number of movies?

Tom London (1883–1963), who appeared in more than 2,000 movies, beginning with *The Great Train Robbery* in 1903. For many years, he was a leading man at Universal; later in his career, he specialized as a B-western sheriff. His last film was *The Lone Texan* (1959).

Who claimed, "I knew Doris Day before she was a virgin"?

Pianist and wit Oscar Levant (1906–1972), after Day became known for her virginal sex farces with Rock Hudson.

Was the child who played Little Ricky on "I Love Lucy" the son of Lucille Ball and Desi Arnaz?

No. Originally, Little Ricky was played by a doll wrapped in a blanket. Later, two six-month-old twins, Richard and Ronald Simmons, took the part, followed by three-year-old twins Michael and Joseph Mayer. The last child to play Little Ricky was Richard Keith, whose real name was Keith Thibodeaux.

How long did "I Love Lucy" run?

Six seasons—from October 15, 1951, to June 24, 1957.

What was Sergeant Joe Friday's badge number on "Dragnet"?

It was number 714.

How many episodes of "The Honeymooners" were filmed? When did they first air?

Thirty-nine half-hour episodes, usually referred to as the Classic 39, were broadcast from October 1955 to September 1956. "The Honeymooners" appeared as a sketch on Jackie Gleason variety shows before and after that series. Reruns of the original 39 episodes continue to be shown.

Where in Brooklyn did the Kramdens and the Nortons live?

They lived at 328 Chauncey Street in the Bensonhurst section of Brooklyn (although the real Chauncey Street is located in Bushwick, Brooklyn).

In the 1956 movie of the same name, what was the Forbidden Planet?

It was called Altair IV.

What was Elvis Presley's first number one hit?

"Heartbreak Hotel" in February 1956. For 16 months following, he had a record—sometimes two—on the nation's Top 10 list.

Where did the Chipmunks in the Chipmunks' "Christmas Song" get their names?

Songwriter and performer David Seville chose the names for the "stars" of his 1958 hit record. Simon and Alvin were named for two executives at Liberty Records—Simon Waronker and Al Bennett. Theodore was named for Ted Keep, the recording engineer.

Where did Chubby Checker get his name?

Born Ernest Evans, Checker chose his stage name as an homage to Fats Domino.

Which movie has won the most Oscars? How many did it win?

Ben-Hur with 11 Oscars is the biggest winner to date.

What was the Nouvelle Vague?

The French New Wave of filmmakers who changed the face of French film in the late 1950s. The group included: Claude Chabrol, François Truffaut, Jean-Luc Godard, Eric Rohmer, and Jacques Rivette. They pioneered a freer, more personal cinematic style that rebelled against standard industry practices. Truffaut's *400 Blows* (1959) and Godard's *Breathless* (1960) are two classic Nouvelle Vague films.

How long did "Howdy Doody" run?

The television series ran from 1947 to 1960.

Who was the voice of Mr. Ed?

Rocky Lane, a cowboy movie hero whose films included: *King of the Mounties*, *Red Gulch Renegades*, and *Silver City Kid*. On at least one occasion, George Burns also supplied Mr. Ed's voice.

In the comic strip "Peanuts," what is Linus and Lucy's last name?

Van Pelt.

What is Charlie Brown's father's profession?

Barber.

What were the earlier names for the Beatles?

There were several. In the late 1950s, John Lennon and Paul McCartney formed a band to play "skiffle" music in local Liverpool clubs. They first called themselves the Quarrymen, then tried several other names: Johnny and the Moondogs, the Moonshiners, Long John and the Silver Beatles. By 1960, however, they settled on the name now known to all—the Beatles.

How many singles did the Beatles release in 1964— their first year?

Twenty-nine:

I Want to Hold Your Hand
She Loves You
Please Please Me
I Saw Her Standing There
My Bonnie (with Tony Sheridan)
From Me to You
Twist and Shout
Roll over Beethoven
All My Loving
Can't Buy Me Love
Do You Want to Know a Secret?
You Can't Do That
Thank You Girl
Love Me Do
There's a Place
Why (with Tony Sheridan)
P.S. I Love You
This Boy
Ain't She Sweet
A Hard Day's Night
I Should Have Known Better
And I Love Her
If I Fell
I'll Cry Instead
I'm Happy Just to Dance with You
Matchbox
Slow Down
I Feel Fine
She's a Woman

As Maria in the 1965 musical *The Sound of Music*, Julie Andrews was described as a *flibbertigibbet*. What is it?

Shakespeare used the word in *King Lear* to describe a devil, and Sir Walter Scott used it in *Kenilworth* to describe a young rascal. But the meaning Rodgers and Hammerstein intended—a talkative or dizzy person—arose in 1549, in a sermon by Bishop Hugh Latimer for King Edward VI. Latimer spelled the word *flybbertgybe*.

How many Perry Mason novels did Erle Stanley Gardner write?

He wrote 75 "case of the" books, beginning with *The Case of the Velvet Claws* in 1933 and ending with *The Case of the Troubled Trustee* in 1965. Gardner died in 1970.

Did 007 have any significance for James Bond beyond representing his "license to kill"?

It was the number of seconds left until the atomic bomb was set to explode in Fort Knox when Bond shut it off in the movie *Goldfinger* (1964).

Which actors have played James Bond?

Sean Connery, George Lazenby, David Niven, Roger Moore, and Timothy Dalton.

How many film versions of *Batman* have there been?

Four. There was *Batman*, a 15-chapter Columbia serial in 1943, with Lewis Wilson in the title role. Then came

Batman and Robin, another Columbia serial in 1949, starring Robert Lowery. In 1966, 20th Century-Fox released a feature film called *Batman* based on the television series and starring Adam West. In 1989, Warner Brothers released *Batman*, starring Michael Keaton.

What did the acronyms U.N.C.L.E. and T.H.R.U.S.H. stand for on "The Man from U.N.C.L.E."?

U.N.C.L.E. was the United Network Command for Law and Enforcement. Its nemesis, T.H.R.U.S.H., was the Technological Hierarchy for the Removal of Undesirables and the Subjugation of Humanity. The television series, starring Robert Vaughn and David McCallum, ran from 1964 to 1967.

On "Star Trek," what was Captain James T. Kirk's middle name?

Tiberius.

On "Star Trek," what were the names of Spock's parents?

Sarek, a Vulcan ambassador, and Amanda, a human being.

How old was Michael Jackson when the Jackson 5 released its first song? What was the song?

Michael Joe Jackson, born August 29, 1958, was eleven when "I Want You Back" was released in November 1969 and sold 2 million copies in its first six weeks.

Where were the Continental Baths, where Barry Manilow and Bette Midler got their start?

The Continental Baths, where Manilow joined Midler in 1970, were located in the basement of the Ansonia Hotel between West Seventy-third and Seventy-fourth Streets in New York City. The club closed several years ago.

Who was the first actor or actress to win three Academy Awards?

By 1940, when the Oscars ceremony was only a dozen years old, character actor Walter Brennan (1894–1974) had already won three Best Supporting Actor awards for his performances in *Come and Get It* (1936), *Kentucky* (1938), and *The Westerner* (1940).

Katharine Hepburn has won four Academy Awards—for Best Actress. Ingrid Bergman won three—two for Best Actress, one for Best Supporting Actress.

Which Hollywood star has played the most leading roles?

John Wayne (1907–1979). He had a leading role in all but 11 of his 153 movies. His career began with *The Drop Kick* in 1927 and ended with *The Shootist* in 1976.

How many Tony Awards has Julie Harris won?

Five—the most Tonys won by any actor or actress. The awards were for her dramatic performances in the following plays:

I Am a Camera (1952)
The Lark (1956)
Forty Carats (1969)
The Last of Mrs. Lincoln (1973)
The Belle of Amherst (1977)

How many actors have played Raymond Chandler's detective Philip Marlowe?

Seven. They are: Dick Powell, Humphrey Bogart, Robert Montgomery, George Montgomery, James Garner, Elliott Gould, and Robert Mitchum. Only Mitchum has played him more than once—in *Farewell My Lovely* (1975) and *The Big Sleep* (1978).

How many actors have played Al Capone?

At least six: Paul Muni, Rod Steiger, Neville Brand, Jason Robards, Ben Gazzara, and Robert DeNiro. Brand played him twice: in *The Scarface Mob* (1959) and *Spin of a Coin* (1962).

What are the stage names of the following people?

Alphonso D'Abruzzo. Robert Alda
Gladys Greene. Jean Arthur
Albert Einstein. Albert Brooks
Richard Jenkins. Richard Burton
Tula Finklea. Cyd Charisse
Lily Chauchoin. Claudette Colbert
Declan McManus. Elvis Costello
Alexandra Zuck. Sandra Dee
Margarita Cansino. Rita Hayworth

Krishna Bhanji. Ben Kingsley
Laszlo Löewenstein. Peter Lorre
Susan Tomaling. Susan Sarandon
Michael Shalhoub. Omar Sharif
Gordon Sumner. Sting

What story has most often been made into a movie?
The story of Cinderella has enjoyed 58 film productions—in cinematic and cartoon form—throughout the world. The first Cinderella movie was made in 1898.

What is the most violent film on record?
The 1984 film *Red Dawn*, directed by John Milius, takes top honors. It contains 134 acts of violence per hour, or 2.23 per minute.

How long was Walter Cronkite a television anchorman for CBS?
Cronkite anchored "The CBS Evening News" from April 16, 1962, to March 6, 1981.

What is the longest-running national television series?
NBC's "Meet the Press" has been running since November 20, 1947. It celebrated its 40th anniversary in 1987.

In screen credits, what is a "best boy"?
The designation refers to an assistant or apprentice to the gaffer (chief electrician) or key grip (head handyman).

Which entertainer is known as the Chairman of the Board?

Singer Frank Sinatra. Former New York Yankee pitcher Whitey Ford also earned the appellation.

What does the Lone Ranger's title *Kemo Sabe* really mean?

As used by Tonto on the radio show "The Lone Ranger," it was intended to mean "faithful friend." But in the Apache tongue it means "white shirt." In Navajo it means "soggy shrub."

• 17 •

THE QUESTION AND ANSWER HALL OF FAME

◆◆◆◆◆

What colors make up a rainbow?
Red, orange, yellow, green, blue, indigo, violet.

Which Brontë sister wrote *Wuthering Heights* and which one wrote *Jane Eyre*?
Charlotte Brontë, the most famous of the Brontë sisters, wrote *Jane Eyre* in 1847; Emily Brontë, whose work is notable for its spirit of passion and rebellion, wrote *Wuthering Heights* in 1848.

What are the names of Santa's reindeer?
Dasher, Dancer, Prancer, Vixen, Comet, Cupid, Donder, and Blitzen. Rudolph the Red-Nosed Reindeer,

arguably the most famous reindeer of all, was a later creation.

How many members are there in the U.S. Senate?

There are two from each state for a total of 100.

How often is a bimonthly meeting held?

Bimonthly meetings are held every two months. Meetings held twice a month are sometimes called bimonthly, but they are more accurately described as semimonthly.

Who wrote, "Oh what a tangled web we weave when first we practice to deceive"?

Sir Walter Scott (1771–1832), not Shakespeare.

What does $E = mc^2$ stand for?

According to Albert Einstein's law on the equivalence of mass and energy, the energy (E) of a quantity of matter is equal to the product of the quantity's mass (m) and the square of the velocity of light (c).

What is the rank of hands in poker?

In order of value, from highest to lowest:

>   Royal Flush
>   Straight Flush
>   Four of a Kind
>   Full House
>   Flush

Straight
Three of a Kind
Two Pairs
One Pair
High Card (No Pair)

Who were the Seven Dwarfs in Disney's *Snow White and the Seven Dwarfs* (1937)?

Named by the studio, not the Brothers Grimm, they were: Bashful, Doc, Dopey, Grumpy, Happy, Sleepy, and Sneezy.

What are the seven deadly sins?

As set forth by scholastic theologian Saint Thomas Aquinas (c. 1225–1274), they are: anger, covetousness, envy, gluttony, lust, pride, and sloth.

What are the seven virtues?

They are: faith, hope, charity (or love), prudence, justice, fortitude, and temperance. The first three are called the theological virtues, the last four the cardinal virtues.

What are the Ten Commandments?

The Ten Commandments vary according to religion and denomination. In the Jewish tradition, the Ten Commandments (based on Exodus 20:2–17 and Deuteronomy 5:6–21) are as follows:

1. I am the Lord your God who brought you out of Egypt, out of the land of slavery.

2. You shall have no other god to set against me. You shall not make a carved image for yourself.

3. You shall not make wrong use of the name of the Lord your God.

4. Remember to keep the Sabbath day holy.

5. Honor your father and your mother.

6. You shall not commit murder.

7. You shall not commit adultery.

8. You shall not steal.

9. You shall not give false evidence against your neighbor.

10. You shall not covet your neighbor's wife; you shall not covet your neighbor's house or anything that belongs to him.

In the Christian tradition, the Jewish first commandment is not included in the list. For Eastern Orthodox Christians and most Protestants, the first and second commandments are as follows:

1. You shall have no other god to set against me.
2. You shall not make a carved image for yourself.

The commandments then continue in conformity with the Jewish tradition. Roman Catholics and Lutherans, however, list the commandments as follows:

1. You shall have no other god to set against me; you shall not make a carved image for yourself.

2. You shall not make wrong use of the name of the Lord your God.
3. Remember to keep the Sabbath day holy.
4. Honor your father and your mother.
5. You shall not commit murder.
6. You shall not commit adultery.
7. You shall not steal.
8. You shall not give false evidence against your neighbor.
9. You shall not covet your neighbor's wife.
10. You shall not covet your neighbor's house or anything that belongs to him.

What are the opening words of the Declaration of Independence?

When in the course of human events it becomes necessary for one people to dissolve the political bands which have connected them with another, and to assume among the powers of the earth, the separate and equal station to which the Laws of Nature and of Nature's God entitle them, a decent respect to the opinions of mankind requires that they should declare the causes which impel them to separation.

What are the five longest rivers?

1. Nile, Africa
2. Amazon, South America
3. Mississippi–Missouri, United States
4. Yangtze, China
5. Ob–Irtysh, USSR

What are the names of the first astronauts to have voyaged to the moon, and which ones set foot on the moon and who stayed in the capsule?

Edwin E. ("Buzz") Aldrin, Jr., Neil Armstrong, and Michael Collins. Collins circled the moon in the capsule while Aldrin and Armstrong landed.

What are the names of the seven original astronauts in the American space program?

M. Scott Carpenter, L. Gordon Cooper, Jr., John H. Glenn, Jr., Virgil I. Grissom, Walter M. Schirra, Jr., Alan B. Shepard, Jr., and Donald K. Slayton.

Who was the lyricist and who was the composer for the Gilbert and Sullivan operettas?

W. S. Gilbert wrote the lyrics and Arthur Sullivan wrote the music.

Who was Richard M. Nixon's running mate in 1960?

Henry Cabot Lodge.

What is the first sentence of Herman Melville's *Moby-Dick*?

"Call me Ishmael."

What are the last words of *A Christmas Carol*?

"And so, as Tiny Tim observed, 'God Bless us, Every One!'"

What are the opening and closing lines to *A Tale of Two Cities?*

The opening line:

> It was the best of times, it was the worst of times, it was the age of wisdom, it was the age of foolishness, it was the epoch of belief, it was the epoch of incredulity, it was the season of Light, it was the season of Darkness, it was the spring of hope, it was the winter of despair, we had everything before us, we had nothing before us, we were all going direct to Heaven, we were all going direct the other way—in short, the period was so far like the present period, that some of its noisiest authorities insisted on its being received, for good or for evil, in the superlative degree of comparison only.

The closing line, spoken by Sydney Carton:

> "It is a far, far better thing that I do, than I have ever done; it is a far, far better rest that I go to than I have ever known."

What were the Seven Wonders of the World and do any of them still exist?

As listed in the second century B.C. by Antipater of Sidon, they were:

1. The Pyramids of Egypt
2. The Hanging Gardens of Babylon
3. The Statue of Zeus at Olympia
4. The Temple of Artemis at Ephesus

5. The Mausoleum at Halicarnassus
6. The Colossus of Rhodes
7. The Pharos (Lighthouse) at Alexandria

Only the pyramids—the oldest of the seven wonders—survive today.

Who were the six wives of Henry VIII?

Catherine of Aragon. Married 1509, divorced 1533; mother of Mary Tudor.
Anne Boleyn. Married 1533, beheaded 1536; mother of Elizabeth I, born 1533.
Jane Seymour. Married 1536, died in childbirth 1537; mother of Edward VI, born 1537.
Anne of Cleves. Married and divorced 1540.
Catherine Howard. Married 1540, beheaded 1542.
Catherine Parr. Married 1543, survived him.

What were the 13 original American colonies?

Connecticut, Delaware, Georgia, Maryland, Massachusetts, New Hampshire, New Jersey, New York, North Carolina, Pennsylvania, Rhode Island, South Carolina, and Virginia.

What are the capitals of each of the 50 states?

State	Capital
Alabama	Montgomery
Alaska	Juneau
Arizona	Phoenix

State	Capital
Arkansas	Little Rock
California	Sacramento
Colorado	Denver
Connecticut	Hartford
Delaware	Dover
Florida	Tallahassee
Georgia	Atlanta
Hawaii	Honolulu
Idaho	Boise
Illinois	Springfield
Indiana	Indianapolis
Iowa	Des Moines
Kansas	Topeka
Kentucky	Frankfort
Louisiana	Baton Rouge
Maine	Augusta
Maryland	Annapolis
Massachusetts	Boston
Michigan	Lansing
Minnesota	Saint Paul
Mississippi	Jackson
Missouri	Jefferson City
Montana	Helena
Nebraska	Lincoln
Nevada	Carson City
New Hampshire	Concord
New Jersey	Trenton
New Mexico	Santa Fe
New York	Albany
North Carolina	Raleigh

State	Capital
North Dakota	Bismarck
Ohio	Columbus
Oklahoma	Oklahoma City
Oregon	Salem
Pennsylvania	Harrisburg
Rhode Island	Providence
South Carolina	Columbia
South Dakota	Pierre
Tennessee	Nashville
Texas	Austin
Utah	Salt Lake City
Vermont	Montpelier
Virginia	Richmond
Washington	Olympia
West Virginia	Charlestown
Wisconsin	Madison
Wyoming	Cheyenne

What is the difference between *deduction* and *induction?*

In the process of *deduction*, you derive conclusions from assumed statements by using the rules of logic—moving from the general to the specific. In *induction*, you make inferences from experiments or observations to build a general law—moving from the specific to the general.

What words end in *gry?*

Angry, hungry, and gry, which is a now obsolete unit of measure that is equal to 0.008 inch.

◆ 18 ◆

RELIGION

◆◆◆◆◆

When was Christ born and how do we know?

He was probably born in 6 B.C. We know because the Bible suggests that Christ was at least two years old when King Herod died. Herod, we know from other sources, died in 4 B.C.

What was the first hotel to have Gideon Bibles?

In November 1908, the Superior Hotel in Iron Mountain, Montana, became the first hotel to have Bibles placed in all its rooms by the Gideons. The Gideons were an organization for Christian business travelers founded in 1899 by Samuel Eugene Hill. By 1975, the Gideons had placed more than 10 million Bibles in hotels, hospitals, and other institutions around the world.

How large was Noah's ark?

It was 300 by 50 by 30 cubits, according to Genesis 6:15. One cubit equals 18 inches.

Are any of the animals on Noah's ark specified in the Bible?

Yes, a raven and a dove. In Genesis 8:7–8, they are the birds Noah sent out to see if the waters had begun to subside:

> And he sent forth a raven, which went to and fro, until the waters were dried up from off the earth. Also he sent forth a dove from him, to see if the waters were abated from off the face of the ground.

Why did Cain have a mark?

Genesis 4:13–15 explains that the mark was placed on Cain to protect him from anyone who might want to kill him in retaliation for his murder of Abel. The mark was not itself meant as a punishment.

What does the name Islam mean?

It is Arabic for "surrender," or "submission," to the will of God. A Muslim is "one who surrenders."

Where is Mecca?

The birthplace of Muhammad lies 45 miles inland from the Red Sea in southwestern Saudi Arabia. Its 300,000 inhabitants are all Muslims; non-Muslims are prohibited. Over 2 million Muslims annually make the pilgrimage to the city.

Who was the first pope? The second? The third?

Peter, one of Jesus' 12 apostles, was the first bishop of the Christian church in Rome—the office now referred to as the papacy. After Peter's execution by the Romans in A.D. 67, Linus became bishop of Rome. Anacletus (also known as Cletus) succeeded him in about A.D. 76.

What are the most popular names for popes?

John, Gregory, Benedict, and Clement, in that order. There have been 23 Johns (and 2 John Pauls), 16 Gregorys, 15 Benedicts, and 14 Clements.

What is the difference between seraphim and cherubim?

In Christian theology, seraphim are the angels nearest to God; cherubim sit just below them. Seraphim have three pairs of wings; cherubim, one or two pairs. There are nine choirs of angels in all. From highest to lowest, they are: seraphim, cherubim, thrones, dominions, virtues, powers, principalities, archangels, and angels.

How many saints does the Catholic Church recognize?

There are about 2,500 saints with feast days, 200 fewer than in the earlier years of the twentieth century. In 1969, the Vatican removed the feast days of over 200 saints from the liturgical calendar because they were of only regional interest or because there were no records of whether the saints had lived. Among the saints affected were Saint Valentine, patron of lovers, and Saint Christopher, patron of travelers.

What is the Immaculate Conception?

It does not refer to Christ's being born of a virgin. Instead, it is the Roman Catholic belief that Mary was without original sin from the moment of her conception.

Where was Gethsemane?

The garden where Jesus was visited by an angel and betrayed by Judas was located on the western slope of the Mount of Olives, east of Jerusalem.

What were the names of the criminals crucified at the same time as Jesus Christ?

Tradition gives the names of the two thieves as Dismas and Gestas. The New Testament does not say.

What was the Bug Bible?

The Bug Bible was the name given to Coverdale's Bible of 1535 because it translated Psalm 91:5 as "Thou shalt not nede to be afrayed for eny bugges by night." The more common translation for the same Hebrew word (for example, in the King James Version) is "terror."

What is the difference between *Brahman* and *Brahmin*?

Brahman is, in Hinduism, the great power of the universe, or "world spirit." In the *Upanishads*, it also refers to a person's spirit. A *Brahmin* is a member of the priesthood, or *varna*, in the Hindu social system.

What are the "ends of man" in Hinduism?

They are the four basic goals of Hinduism:

> *Dharma.* Religious Duty
> *Artha.* Earthly Gain

Kama. Physical Pleasure
Moksha. Spiritual Liberation

What are the eight elements of the Buddhist Eightfold Path?

These are the eight elements that the Buddha thought were essential to enlightenment and liberation. They are: right views, right intention, right speech, right action, right livelihood, right effort, right mindfulness, and right concentration.

What does the word *avatar* mean to a Hindu?

It means the human incarnation of a god. The word is most frequently applied to the 10 incarnations of Vishnu, the benevolent god of sun and light. His most famous avatars are: Krishna, Rama, and Buddha.

Who are the Four Horsemen of the Apocalypse?

These personifications of war appear in the Book of Revelation 6:1–8. They are: Conquest, Slaughter, Famine, and Death, riding horses that are, respectively, white, red, black, and green.

What were the 10 plagues of Egypt?

As outlined in Exodus 7–12 and recounted every year in the Passover ritual, the plagues God sent to free the Jews from bondage in Egypt were:

1. The Waters Turned to Blood
2. The Frogs

3. The Gnats (or Lice)
4. The Flies
5. The Pestilence (murrain, which killed the cattle)
6. The Boils
7. The Hail
8. The Locusts
9. The Darkness
10. The Death of the First-Born Egyptians

What was the original meaning of the word *scapegoat*?

As described in Leviticus 16:1–27, part of a Hebrew ritual on the Day of Atonement involved the presentation of two male goats at the altar of the tabernacle. After lots were cast, one goat was sacrificed to the Lord; the other, the *scapegoat*, was set aside for Azazel, an evil spirit of the wilderness. The high priest transferred the sins of the people onto this goat and sent it away into the desert.

Is there anything in astronomy that might correspond to the Star of Bethlehem?

No comets, novae, or supernovae are recorded for 6 B.C., the estimated year of Christ's birth. But there was one odd celestial event that stargazing Wise Men might have observed: Mars, Jupiter, and Saturn came close together in a small triangle, as they do once every 805 years.

When was hymn-singing introduced into Christian churches?

Ambrose, bishop of Milan, introduced hymn-singing in A.D. 386.

> *When was incense introduced?*
> Incense was introduced in A.D. 500.

What are the canonical hours?

They are times of day set aside for prayer. As specified by church regulations, the divisions of the day are: matins, lauds, prime, terce, sext, none, vespers, and compline.

Which religion uses a prayer wheel?

Tibetan Buddhists developed the prayer wheel as a substitute for the repeated recitation of *mantras* (syllables or verses of mystical power). The wheel is a hollow metal cylinder mounted on a rod, with the *mantra* written on a roll of paper inside the cylinder. The Buddhist turns the wheel by hand; each turn is believed to have a spiritual effect equivalent to reciting the prayer orally. Prayer wheels are sometimes mounted on windmills and watermills, where natural forces can, in effect, be put to work "reciting" the *mantra*.

Which religion uses prayer rugs?

Muslims of central and western Asia use prayer rugs to cover the ground while they pray. The rugs feature a distinctive arch-shaped design—a prayer niche, or *mihrāb*—on one end of the carpet. The *mihrāb* must be pointed toward Mecca while the person is praying.

Who invented the rosary?

The practice of using a string of knots or beads as a memory aid in prayer, developed long before the time of Christ, was popularized among Catholics in the twelfth century by Saint Dominic of Spain, founder of the Dominican order. The word *rosary* may come from one of two sources: the early practice of carving rosary beads from rosewood (and calling them "wreaths of roses"); or the French word for bead, *rosaire*.

What is the formal name for the Shakers?

The official name of the celibate sect is the United Society of Believers in Christ's Second Appearing. Derived from the Quakers, the "Shaking Quaker" sect was established in America in 1774 by Ann Lee and reached its height in the 1840s with a membership of 6,000. *Shaker* refers to the involuntary movements made by believers during spells of religious fervor. Only a handful of elderly Shakers survive today.

How many churches in the United States ordain women?

As of the early 1980s, there were seven: the United Methodist Church, the United Presbyterian Church, the United Church of Christ, the Episcopal Church, the Lutheran Church in America, the American Lutheran Church, and the Southern Baptist Convention.

Does Freemasonry have anything to do with stone masonry?

The secret fraternal order of Free and Acceptable Masons has its origins in communities of actual stone-workers—the masons who built cathedrals in the Middle Ages. Eventually, lodges in need of new members started admitting nonmasons, and from these lodges modern Freemasonry developed.

From what day do Muslims calculate their calendar?

Friday, July 16, A.D. 622. This was the day that Muhammad and his early followers made their *hijrah*, or emigration, from Mecca to Medina. They were forced to leave Mecca because of opposition to Muhammad's teachings.

When was the Ark of the Covenant last seen?

The wooden chest that contained God's laws as presented to Moses was taken on its last trip to Jerusalem by King David. Eventually King Solomon put it in the Temple. It disappeared when the Temple was destroyed in 586 B.C.

How old is the Mishnah? How old is the Talmud?

Parts of the Mishnah—a compilation of oral law—date back to earliest Jewish history. The Mishnah was completed by about A.D. 200. The Talmud, which records academic discussion and judicial thought, consists of two parts: the Mishnah and the Gemara, a commentary on the Mishna. The Palestinian Talmud was completed by about A.D. 400; the Babylonian Talmud was finished by A.D. 750.

Who founded Hasidism?

The Jewish spiritual movement was founded by Israel ben Eliezer, now better known as the Ba'al Shem Tov (Master of the Good Name). He was a healer and holy man who lived in the Ukraine (c. 1700–1760).

Can a Jew be excommunicated?

Yes. The Hebrew word for excommunication is *herem*; it involves the cutting of all religious, social, and business ties with someone considered dangerous to the community. One of the most famous cases of *herem* involved the seventeenth-century Dutch philosopher Spinoza.

What is *Gehenna* and what does it have to do with hellfire?

Gehenna is the Greek form of the Hebrew *Ge Hinnom*, or "Valley of Hinnom." This was a valley west and south of Jerusalem where children were sacrificed in flames to the Ammonite god Moloch from the tenth through seventh centuries B.C. In Jewish and Christian thought, it became another name for the place where the wicked burn after death. It is mentioned in both the New Testament and the Talmud.

Where is nirvana? Is it anywhere near Valhalla?

Nirvana is not a place but a state of bliss to which Buddhists aspire. In Sanskrit it means the "going out" of a light. Early Buddhists used the word to describe the extinction of the fires of cravings. Valhalla, in Norse mythology, is the heavenly hall of slain heroes. It also represents a state of bliss—but one in which the dead feast and fight each other for sport.

· 19 ·

ROYALTY AND WORLD LEADERS

•••••

When was Solomon king?

The son of and successor to David is said to have ruled during the mid-tenth century B.C.

Which five rulers reigned the longest?

With their periods of reign, they are:

1. *Pepi II, king of Egypt.* 90 years (c. 2566–2476 B.C.)
2. *Louis XIV, king of France.* 72 years (1643–1715)
3. *John II, prince of Liechtenstein.* 71 years (1858–1929)
4. *Franz Joseph, emperor of Austria.* 68 years (1848–1916)

5. *Victoria, queen of England.* 64 years (1837–1901)

Which world leaders bore the following nicknames?

The Liberator. Simón Bolívar (1783–1830), leader in the quest for Latin American independence; also, Daniel O'Connell (1775–1847), Irish nationalist leader in the British House of Commons.
The Hammer. Charles Martel (688–741?), Frankish ruler who stopped the Muslim invasion of Europe.
The Upright. Abu Bakr (c. 573–634), the first Muslim caliph and successor to Muhammad.
Mr. Republican. Robert Alphonso Taft (1889–1953), U.S. senator from Ohio, son of William Howard Taft, and coauthor of the Taft-Hartley Labor Act.

How far did Alexander the Great's empire reach?

By the time of his death in 323 B.C., Alexander III, king of Macedonia, had conquered Persia, Syria, Phoenicia, Egypt, Bactria, Bukhara, and the Punjab. His armies marched as far as India. He was thirty-three when he died.

How many King Herods were there?

Four. Herod the Great was the tetrarch, or subordinate ruler, of the Roman province of Judaea from 41 B.C. to 4 B.C.; he was probably in power when Jesus Christ was born. Between 4 B.C. and A.D. 34, three sons of Herod the Great—Herod Archelaus, Herod Antipas, and Philip—ruled as ethnarchs. Herod Archelaus died in A.D. 6; Herod Antipas, who died about A.D. 40, was in power when Jesus was crucified. Herod Agrippa I, grandson of Herod the Great, ruled from A.D. 40 to 44.

What is a shogun?

The shoguns were the de facto rulers of Japan from 1192 to 1867. Originally military commanders, they exercised real power, while the emperor retained formal sovereignty. The name is an abbreviation of *sei-i-tai-shōgun*, meaning "barbarian-quelling generalissimo."

When did Genghis Khan live? How far did his reign extend?

Genghis Khan was born circa 1162 and died in 1227. His real name was Temüjin; the title Genghis Khan meant "universal ruler." He ruled Mongolia, conquered China, devastated the Muslim empire of Khwārizm (now part of Soviet Uzbekistan), and raided Persia and Russia.

How are Kublai Khan and Genghis Khan related?

Genghis Khan (c. 1162–1227) was the grandfather of Kublai Khan (1215–1294).

When was the post of Prince of Wales created?

In 1301, when the future Edward II became the first English Prince of Wales. Since then, with some exceptions, the heir apparent to the throne of Great Britain has held the title Prince of Wales.

Who were the doges of Venice?

They were elected dukes who ruled the city-state of Venice and controlled much of the eastern Mediterranean coast. Their reigns tended to be short—often 1 to 10 years. Venice was an independent city-state from 697 until 1797, when Napoleon conquered it.

In the British line of peerage, which is more important, a baron or an earl?

The earl ranks higher, but is by no means at the top. From highest to lowest, the line of peerage runs as follows:

> Duke and Duchess
> Marquess (or Marquis) and Marchioness
> Earl and Countess
> Viscount and Viscountess
> Baron and Baroness

Who was Tamburlaine the Great and when did he live?

He was an Islamic Turkic conqueror born in what is now Soviet Uzbekistan in 1336. By 1400, he and his nomad warriors had conquered the whole area from Mongolia to the Mediterranean. He died in 1405 while on his way to conquer China. Known to historians as Timur Lenk, he is best known to students of literature as the hero of Christopher Marlowe's 1590 tragedy *Tamburlaine the Great*.

Who was the last Byzantine emperor?

Constantine XI, who ruled from 1448 to 1453. He died fighting the Turks in the battle for Constantinople, which ended in the fall of the nearly 1,100-year-old Byzantine Empire.

Who built Buckingham Palace?

It was built by the Duke of Buckingham in 1703 and became the London residence of British royalty in 1837.

How did Catherine the Great die?

She was alone on the morning of November 17, 1796, when she collapsed with a stroke. Earlier that morning, she had bid farewell to a lover—a twenty-seven-year-old man. No horses were involved.

Did King George III really go insane?

Yes. The English king (1738–1820) probably suffered from an inherited blood disorder called porphyria, which affects the nervous system. In 1788, he became violently insane and had to be put in a straitjacket. He recovered but eventually suffered a relapse. After 1811, his son, the future George IV, served as regent.

Was Victoria related to King George III?

Victoria, who reigned from 1837 to 1901, was the granddaughter of the King George III, who lost the

American colonies. This makes Elizabeth II, Queen of England since 1952, George's great-great-great-great-granddaughter.

Who was the longest-reigning pope?

Pius IX, who led the Catholic Church for nearly 32 years, from 1846 to 1878. It was during his reign that the First Vatican Council, in 1870, promulgated the dogma of papal infallibility. That doctrine states that the pope cannot err on matters of faith or morals when speaking ex cathedra, that is, in his official character of supreme pontiff.

Who was the last emperor of China?

Henry Pu-yi, from 1908 to 1912. From 1934 to 1945, he was emperor of the Japanese puppet state of Manchukuo in Manchuria. He died in 1967 in the People's Republic of China.

Which world leader was known as the Conquering Lion?

Haile Selassie (1891–1975), emperor of Ethiopia from 1930 to 1974. His tenacity against his enemies earned him his nickname, a variation of one of his official titles, the Lion of Judah.

When did King Edward VIII abdicate?

Edward VIII gave up his throne for the love of Wallis Warfield Simpson on December 10, 1936.

Who took the throne in his place?
His younger brother George VI, who reigned until 1952, when Elizabeth II became queen.

Who was the first member of British royalty to visit the United States?

It took the New York World's Fair and imminent war in Europe to bring British royalty across the Atlantic. On June 7, 1939, King George VI and the future Queen Elizabeth II crossed the border from Canada to Niagara Falls, then traveled to Washington, D.C., for lunch with President Franklin D. Roosevelt. Later they went to New York City to see the World's Fair and the "World of Tomorrow."

What is the head of the British Secret Service called?

C or CSS. He is not called M—his name in the James Bond stories—although the head of the SOE (Special Operations Executive) in World War II was called M for a while.

Whatever happened to Leon Trotsky?

The one-time foreign minister and war minister of the Soviet Union was expelled from Russia by Joseph Stalin in 1929. He made his way to Mexico, where he was murdered—probably at Stalin's command—in 1940.

Who was the last viceroy of India?

It was not Lord Mountbatten. Louis Mountbatten (1900–1979) was India's last British viceroy, or governor-general, from August 1947 to June 1948. Chakravarti Rajagopalachari (1879–1972) then served as governor-general of India's interim government from June 1948 to January 1950, when the position was abolished.

What was David Ben-Gurion's nationality? What was Golda Meir's?

David Ben-Gurion was born in Poland in 1886. He fled Poland in 1905 and settled in Palestine, becoming the first prime minister of Israel in 1948. Golda Meir was born in Russia in 1898 but was raised in the United States, where her parents moved in 1900. She settled in Palestine in 1921, becoming Israel's fifth prime minister in 1969.

◆ 20 ◆

SCIENCE

◆◆◆◆◆

How old is the moon?

The oldest moon material brought back to earth by the Apollo program crews has been soil-dated to 4.72 billion years.

How large is the moon?

Its diameter is 2,160 miles. The earth's diameter at the equator is 7,926.68 miles.

How hot is the sun?

At its surface, the sun is about 7,640 degrees Fahrenheit. In the sun's interior, temperatures can range above 18 million degrees Fahrenheit.

How fast does the earth travel around the sun?

It moves at 66,641 miles per hour.

If the moon passes between the earth and the sun every month, why doesn't it eclipse the sun?

The orbit of the moon around the earth is tilted at an angle of about 6 degrees from the plane of the earth's orbit around the sun. As a result, the moon is usually above or below the line between the earth and the sun—except on certain predictable occasions.

How long is a cosmic year?

A cosmic year is the length of time it takes the sun to complete one revolution around the center of the Milky Way galaxy—about 225 million earth years. The sun is between 20 and 21 cosmic years old.

How fast is continental drift?

The plates (solid segments of the earth's crust and upper mantle) that consist mostly of continents move at an average speed of about 2 centimeters per year. Europe and North America are moving apart at about this speed. The plates that are mostly under the oceans move faster, at an average speed of about 10 centimeters per year. It has been 200 million years since the original supercontinent, Pangaea, broke up into the continents we know today.

What is the pressure at the bottom of the Pacific Ocean?

At the Pacific Ocean's greatest depth—36,198 feet (in the Marianas trench southwest of Guam)—the pressure is 16,124 pounds per square inch, more than

1,000 times the atmospheric pressure at sea level (14.7 pounds per square inch).

What is the continental shelf?

It is an underwater ledge around the coastline of the world's oceans. The edge of the shelf lies at depths of between 360 and 480 feet. The width may vary from a few feet to several hundred miles.

How many types of clouds are there?

There are 10: cirrus, cirrocumulus, cirrostratus, altocumulus, altostratus, nimbostratus, stratocumulus, stratus, cumulus, cumulonimbus. Each of these clouds has a different shape and internal structure.

When do scientists believe the earth formed?

4.6 billion years ago.

What is the earliest era of geologic time?

It is the Precambrian age, which began when the earth's crust formed, 4.6 billion years ago, and ended with the dawn of the Cambrian period, 570 million years ago. About seven-eighths of earth's history since the formation of the crust took place during the Precambrian age.

In what geologic era did man evolve?

In the Pleistocene epoch, which began about 2.5 million years ago and ended about 10,000 years ago.

In what era do we live now?

The Recent (or Holocene) epoch, beginning about 10,000 years ago.

When are dinosaurs said to have become extinct?

Dinosaurs lived during the Mesozoic era, 225 million to 65 million years ago. By the close of that era, all Archosauria (or "ruling reptiles"), except crocodiles, had died.

What is the world's largest plant?

It is said to be the General Sherman Tree, a giant sequoia in Sequoia National Park, California. The tree is about 272 feet tall and more than 100 feet in circumference. It is about 3,500 years old.

What is Saint Elmo's fire?

Named for the patron saint of sailors, the "fire" is actually discharges of electricity that occur during storms; these discharges are seen as blue or bluish white lights at the tips of masts and bowsprits of ships at sea, as well as on church steeples and building spires on land.

How thick is the crust of the earth?

Sometimes likened to the shell that covers an egg, the layer of rock that covers the surface of the earth is, on average, 22 miles thick.

How many species of grasses are there?

There are about 6,000 to 10,000 species of "true" grasses—members of the family Poaceae. They are the most widespread and numerous of all the flowering plants.

What's the difference between a *stalagmite* and a *stalactite*?

Both are elongated deposits of minerals at points where slowly dripping water enters a void. *Stalagmites* build from the bottom of such a cavity; *stalactites* hang from the ceiling. When the same dripwater source creates both a stalactite and a stalagmite, the two may meet and form a column.

How much does lightning heat the atmosphere?

An average bolt raises the air temperature along its way to 50,000 degrees Fahrenheit.

When were the planets discovered?

Mercury, Mars, Venus, Jupiter, and Saturn were known from ancient times. Uranus was discovered in 1781, Neptune in 1846, and Pluto in 1930.

What makes a wave break?

It occurs when the water that supports a wave is only about 1.3 times as deep as the wave is high. At that point, the water at the crest is moving faster than the water below. This condition commonly occurs in shallow water at the shore, but it may occur farther off if the wave is high enough.

What causes hail?

Hailstones begin as frozen raindrops or pellets of snow in a thunderstorm cloud. These "hail embryos" are

carried by updrafts to a part of the storm where droplets of water exist in a supercooled state (that is, in
liquid form at temperatures below freezing). These
supercooled droplets freeze into ice when they strike
the surface of the hail embryo. As the ice accumulates,
the embryo grows into a hailstone. It continues to
grow larger the longer it stays among the supercooled
droplets. As the hailstone gets heavier, it falls, but other
air currents carry it back up. Eventually the hailstone
becomes too heavy to be supported, and it falls to the
ground.

How many stars can you see on a clear night?

At any given time on a clear night in a dark place with
no obstructions on the horizon, 2,500 stars are visible
to the naked eye.

How many stars are too faint to be seen?

In our galaxy alone, there are about 100 billion stars. In
the universe that we can see, the number of stars is
estimated at 10^{22}.

What are shooting stars?

They are not stars but meteorites—particles from space
entering and burning up in the earth's atmosphere.

Who first said "Eureka!" and what did it have to do with a bath?

The Greek word *heureka*, meaning "I have found it,"
was made famous by Archimedes, a Sicilian philosopher (c. 287–212 B.C.). Archimedes was given the task

of finding out whether a crown presented to the ruler of Syracuse was really pure gold or alloyed with an inferior metal. The philosopher was baffled until he stepped into his bath and noticed it overflowing. He realized that objects of equal weight but different density displace different amounts of water when immersed—the principle of specific gravity. Since gold has a different density than other metals, immersion in water could be used to determine whether the crown was made of pure gold. The idea excited Archimedes so much that he jumped out of the public bath shouting *"Heureka! Heureka!"*—then ran home naked to try the experiment.

When was Halley's comet first spotted?

Chinese astronomers made the first recorded observation in 240 B.C.

> ### What does Halley have to do with it?
> In 1705, English astronomer Edmund Halley was the first to theorize that comets travel in regular orbits around the sun. Proposing that "the great comet" observed in 1682 made periodic visits about every 76 years, he predicted that it would return in 1758. The comet was named for him when his prediction came true, 16 years after his death.

When was the first leap year?

The first leap year was 46 B.C. It was then that the Julian calendar of 365.25 days was adopted. The calendar required that an extra day be added every fourth year.

What kind of calendar do we use—the Julian or the Gregorian?

Most of the world's non-Muslim countries use the Gregorian calendar, introduced by Pope Gregory XIII in 1582 as a reform of the Julian calendar. (The latter, instituted by Julius Caesar, had been in use since 46 B.C.) Americans have used the Gregorian calendar since 1752.

What's the difference?

The principal difference between the two calendars is that in the Gregorian system a century year must be divisible by 400 in order to qualify as a leap year (e.g., A.D. 2000 is a leap year but not A.D. 1900). For each century that is not divisible by 400, the Julian calendar falls one day behind the Gregorian calendar. Thus, by 1542, October 4 on the Julian calendar was equivalent to October 15 on the Gregorian calendar.

What is Newton's law of gravity?

Actually called Newton's law of gravitation, it describes the degree to which one body of matter attracts another. That attraction is in direct proportion to the product of the bodies' masses, and in inverse proportion to the square of the distance between them. This law can be expressed in a formula first set forth in 1687:

$$F = G \frac{(m_1 \, m_2)}{R^2}$$

(F is the attractive force; G is the gravitational constant, 6.67×10^{-8} dyne·cm^2/gm^2; m_1 and m_2 are the two masses; R^2 is the distance squared.)

Generations of schoolchildren have ignored the formula and remembered, "Whatever goes up must come down."

If 32 degrees is the freezing point of water on the Fahrenheit scale, what does 0 degrees represent?

German physicist Gabriel Daniel Fahrenheit (1686–1736) took the temperature of an equal ice-salt mixture as the zero for his scale.

Was there ever a planet Vulcan?

Astronomers once believed that a planet called Vulcan existed between the planet Mercury and the sun. Its existence—first proposed by French astronomer Urbain Jean Joseph Leverrier in 1845—was hypothesized to explain a discrepancy in Mercury's orbit. Vulcan was even reported to have been observed once, but the observation was never confirmed. Einstein's general theory of relativity later explained Mercury's odd orbit, and the existence of Vulcan was discredited.

What is the difference between brass and bronze?

Brass is an alloy of copper and zinc. Bronze is a more durable mixture of copper and tin.

What does it mean to galvanize steel?

It means that a zinc coating is applied, either by "hot-dipping" the steel in molten zinc or by electroplating it in an electrolytic process. Thus protected against exposure, galvanized iron or steel is less liable to rust.

What does saltpeter do?

Contrary to dormitory fears, it does not inhibit sexual desire. Instead, saltpeter, or potassium nitrate (KNO_3), is a diuretic. Another form of saltpeter is Chile saltpeter, or impure sodium nitrate ($NaNO_3$). Lime, or Norwegian saltpeter, is calcium nitrate. It is used to make explosives.

Who discovered the speed of light?

The first to approximate it roughly was French physicist Armand Fizeau (1819–1896), who in 1849 obtained a value for the speed of light that was about 5 percent too high. Fizeau's contemporary Jean Foucault (1819–1868) obtained the first accurate measurement (within 1 percent of the correct speed) in 1862.

Who came up with the phrase *survival of the fittest*?

Not Charles Darwin. The British philosopher and scientist Herbert Spencer introduced the phrase in *Principles of Biology* (1864–1867) as a way of describing Darwin's theory of natural selection.

How does quicksand work?

Not by pulling you down. Quicksand is nearly always found above a spring, which creates a supersaturated condition that makes the sand frictionless and unable to support weight. In addition, quicksand is airless, which creates suction as you struggle to get free. The most effective way to escape quicksand is to position yourself on top of it and "roll" out.

Is typhoid fever the same thing as typhus?

No. Typhus is caused by microbes called rickettsiae and is carried by fleas, mites, and ticks, which in turn are carried by rats and other rodents. Typhoid (also called typhoid fever or enteric fever) resembles typhus in its symptoms but is caused by a different microbe, *Salmonella typhi*, which is usually carried by food or water contaminated with human feces. Both diseases cause fever, delirium, rashes, and coughs.

What is avoirdupois weight?

It is the system we use whenever we measure a grain, dram (27.3 grains), ounce (16 drams), or pound (16 ounces).

What is glass made of?

It is generally made of three components: silica, in the form of sand; an alkali flux, such as soda or potash, which promotes fusion; and lime, which stabilizes the mixture. In the process of being heated and then cooled, glass loses its crystalline nature and becomes an amorphous but rigid substance. Like a solid, it is stiff enough to keep its shape. But like a liquid, the spacing of its molecules is wide enough for the glass to be transparent.

Which hurricane in the United States took the most lives?

In 1900, a hurricane in Galveston, Texas, with 15- to 20-foot waves swept over Galveston Island and drowned 6,000 people.

What makes noble gases *noble*?

The term refers to the lack of chemical reactivity in these inert gases. For the record, there are six noble gases: helium, neon, argon, krypton, xenon, and radon.

Where did Freud get the term *id*?

Sigmund Freud's original term for the unconscious mind was not *id* but *es*—the indefinite pronoun *it* in German. Freud borrowed that term from a physician, Georg Groddick, who in turn had borrowed it from his teacher Ernst Schweninger. As Freud's ideas became popular in English-speaking countries, translators felt that simply calling the unconscious *it* was too vague and unscientific. They replaced *it* with its Latin translation—*id*.

Why did George Washington Carver study the peanut?

The scientist (1864–1943) was trying to find ways to diversify southern agriculture. Long dependent on cotton, the South's economy was threatened by the boll weevil and depleted soil. Carver showed that the neglected peanut, soybean, and sweet potato could produce hundreds of trade goods and replace soil minerals depleted by cotton. The South's economy was revolutionized as a result.

What are polymers? Are they the same thing as plastics?

Plastics are only one kind of polymer—a substance composed of very large chainlike molecules that consist of smaller, repeating chemical units. Natural polymers include proteins, cellulose, diamonds, and quartz. Besides plastics, manmade ones include concrete, glass, and paper.

What led Albert Einstein to remark, "I shall never believe that God plays dice with the universe"?

It was brought on by the awarding of the 1932 Nobel Prize in physics to Werner Heisenberg for his uncertainty principle—the principle that you cannot accurately know both the position and momentum of an atomic particle at the same time. Einstein believed that the principle made a mockery of cause and effect.

Who named the quark?

American physicist Murray Gell-Mann (b. 1929) in 1964. He took the name from James Joyce's *Finnegans Wake*. A quark, a subatomic particle with a fractional electric charge, is believed by physicists to be the fundamental unit of matter.

How much is the number *googol*?

First used in 1940 by nine-year-old Milton Sirotta, it is the number 1 followed by 100 zeros. It was brought to public attention by Sirotta's uncle, mathematician Edward Kasner, in his book *Mathematics and the Imagination*.

Who developed the lobotomy?

The prefrontal lobotomy was invented by Portuguese surgeon António Caetano de Abreu Freire Egas Moniz

(1874–1955) for patients with incurable mental disturbances. Moniz, who also served as the foreign minister of Portugal from 1918 to 1919, was awarded the Nobel Prize in physiology or medicine in 1949.

How much energy does a supernova generate?

The explosion of a star is estimated to release 10^{49} ergs—1 followed by 49 zeros. By comparison, pronouncing an average syllable releases 200 ergs, and the first atom bomb produced 10^{21} ergs.

Who came up with the term *black hole* and what is it?

Twentieth-century American physicist John Archibald Wheeler (b. 1911) coined the term to describe a collapsed star whose gravitational field is so intense that not even light can escape from it.

Do diamonds burn?

Yes, if you heat them to somewhere between 1,400 to 1,607 degrees Fahrenheit. A blowtorch will do the trick. Diamonds are composed of pure carbon and will convert into graphite under such temperatures.

What is a quasar?

It is another name for a quasi-stellar object. It looks like a star but emits as much radiation as an entire galaxy, with a volume far smaller than that of our Milky Way galaxy. No one knows what a quasar is; recent evidence suggests it might be a galaxy with a big black hole at the center.

What are neutrinos?

Neutrinos are objects produced by the decay of certain subatomic particles. They have energy but little or no mass, and they travel almost at the speed of light.

What is the chemical content of guano?

Bird guano—the accumulated excrement and remains of birds such as cormorants, pelicans, and gannets—is 11 to 16 percent nitrogen, 8 to 12 percent phosphoric acid, and 2 to 3 percent potash. The excellent fertilizer is harvested from islands off Peru, Baja California, and Africa. Bat and seal guano is also highly prized.

How do nonchlorine "fabric brighteners" make clothes brighter?

A common ingredient in many laundry detergents, optical bleaches ("fabric brighteners") act by reflecting blue light. The blue light combines with the yellow discoloration in a fabric to produce white light that makes the fabric seem brighter.

What are close encounters of the first and second kind?

The first kind is the sighting of UFOs. The second is the finding of physical evidence of UFOs. A close encounter of the third kind is actual physical contact with UFOs.

What does the term *plasma* mean to a physician?

The fluid part of blood, lymph, or milk as distinct from suspended matter.

To a physicist?
A collection of negatively charged electrons and positively charged ions, existing in about equal numbers in a neutral state; plasma is considered a fourth state of matter, distinct from gases, liquids, and solids.

To a geologist?
A kind of quartz—green, faintly translucent, semiprecious—and a variety of chalcedony.

When a new drug is being tested, what is the difference between a blind test and a double-blind test?

In a blind test of a new drug, the subject does not know if he or she is receiving the drug or a placebo, but the physician administering the test does know. In a double-blind test, neither the subject nor the physician knows.

What makes houseplants turn toward the light?

Growth hormones called auxins. When light falls on one side of a plant, the auxins tend to concentrate on the shaded side, causing the cells on that side to grow longer. As a result, the plant gradually leans toward the light. This bending movement in response to an outside stimulus is known as tropism; bending in response to sunlight is called heliotropism.

What makes a firefly give off light?

The light comes from an area on the sides of its stomach. Fatty tissue located there contains air tubes and nerves that when stimulated give off oxygen. The oxygen combines with a pigment in the fat called luciferin, producing the familiar heatless light.

⋄ 21 ⋄

SPORTS

◆◆◆◆◆

When was the first gladiatorial combat?

The first known gladiatorial contest took place in Rome in 264 B.C.; it featured three pairs of armed fighters. Later contests featured hundreds or even thousands of pairs of duelists.

> *When was the last fight?*
> It isn't certain. Constantine abolished the shows in A.D. 325, but they persisted. Honorius abolished them again in the fifth century, but even then they may have continued.

Who invented the boxing glove?

Jack Broughton of Great Britain. The English bare-knuckle fighting champion for many years (beginning in 1734), Broughton also wrote the first set of boxing rules.

When could you have taken part in the sport of gouging?

The frontier sport, imported from England, flourished in the Ohio River Valley around 1800. The object was to gouge out the opponent's eye with a thumbnail. To compete effectively, you would have needed to let your thumbnail grow extra-long.

Where and when was the first recorded baseball game?

On June 19, 1846, at Elysian Fields in Hoboken, New Jersey, the New York Club beat the Knickerbockers, 23–1. On that date, another baseball tradition began: The New York Club pitcher, James Whyte Davis, was fined 6 cents for swearing at the umpire.

Why is the seventh-inning stretch held in the seventh inning?

The practice, which takes place before the home team comes to bat, became popular in 1860 because the number seven is considered lucky.

Where did the baseball term *texas leaguer* come from?

This phrase for a weak hit falling just over the heads of the infielders may first have been used to describe the hits of Arthur Sunday, a player from Texas. Another version is that the term was coined in Syracuse, New York, in 1886 by a pitcher who lost a game because of these short hits—all made by former Houston athletes.

Who won the last legal bare-knuckle bout?

John L. Sullivan knocked out Jake Kilrain in the 75th round of the U.S. heavyweight championship at Richburg, Mississippi, on July 8, 1889. He claimed to have won the world's championship with that victory, since Kilrain had previously fought a draw with the English champion. After that fight, boxing with gloves became the rule.

Who won the first world heavyweight boxing championship using the Marquis of Queensberry rules?

The first world heavyweight boxing championship using gloves and the Queensberry rules took place in New Orleans on September 7, 1892, between James J. Corbett and John L. Sullivan. Corbett knocked out Sullivan in the 21st round.

What is the Baltimore chop?

The term, which came into vogue in 1890, refers to a batted ball that bounces so high that it cannot be fielded successfully before the batter reaches first base. It is said to have been named for two Baltimore players—John McGraw and Willie ("Wee Willie") Keeler—who often reached base this way.

Who won the first Army–Navy football game?

The Navy, 24–0. The game was played at West Point, New York, on November 29, 1890.

Who was the first pro football player?

It was William ("Pudge") Heffelfinger, who made his professional debut for the Allegheny Athletic Association on November 12, 1892. He was paid $500 for his performance against the Pittsburgh Athletic Club, in which he led his team to victory, 4–0.

How far is the pitching mound from home plate?

According to 1894 baseball rules, the 4-by-12-inch pitching rubber embedded in the pitcher's mound lies 60 feet, 6 inches from the front edge of home plate. The pitcher is supposed to place both feet on the rubber at the start of his delivery. Previously, the distance of the mound from home plate had been 50 feet.

What games were played in the first modern Olympics?

The first modern Olympics, held in Athens, Greece, in April 1896, featured the following sports: cycling, fencing, gymnastics, shooting, swimming (including diving, synchronized swimming, water polo), track and field, weight lifting, and wrestling.

Who won the first World Series?

The Boston Red Sox beat the Pittsburgh Pirates five games to three (in what was then a best-of-nine series), October 1 to 13, 1903.

How did the Brooklyn Dodgers get their name?

Dodgers was an abbreviation for *trolley dodgers*. The term developed during the early to mid-twentieth century, when trolley cars were common sights in urban areas such as Brooklyn. To be a trolley dodger meant that you were able to slip through traffic. The players on the field needed the same kind of agility.

Who was the first black man to become heavyweight champion?

Jack Johnson on December 26, 1908. He remained the champion until April 5, 1915, when Jess Willard defeated him in Havana, Cuba.

When was the first Indianapolis 500?

The 500-mile race was first held on May 30, 1911, when Ray Harroun won in 6 hours, 42 minutes, 8 seconds. His average speed was 74.59 miles per hour.

What was the worst disaster in sports history?

More lethal than any soccer riot was the collapse of the grandstands of the Hong Kong Jockey Club on February 26, 1916. In all, 606 racetrack spectators died; hundreds more were injured.

When was the NFL organized?

The National Football League was founded in 1920 in Canton, Ohio. Originally called the American Professional Football Association, it adopted its name in 1922. Athlete Jim Thorpe was its first president. The NFL and the American Football League merged in 1970 to create the new 26-team NFL.

When did Dempsey go through the ropes?

Jack Dempsey was punched through the ropes by a first-round right from Luis Firpo on September 4, 1923, at the Polo Grounds in New York City. The punch did not end the fight: Dempsey came back to win by a knockout in the second round.

How long did it take Gertrude Ederle to swim the English Channel?

The first woman to cross the channel clocked in at 14 hours, 39 minutes on August 5, 1926. In doing so, she broke the existing men's record.

Has any golfer won the prestigious grand slam?

Only Bobby Jones has achieved that feat—and he did so as an amateur, before the present-day tournament requirements were instituted. He won the British Amateur tournament in Scotland on May 31, 1930. Next, on June 20, 1930, he won the British Open in Holyoke, England, with a four-round total of 291. On July 12, he won the U.S. Open in Minneapolis, Minnesota, with a four-round total of 287. Finally, on September 27, in Ardmore, Pennsylvania, he won the U.S. Amateur championship. Despite this accomplishment, Bobby Jones never became a professional golfer. Since World War II, the grand slam has consisted of the U.S. Open, the Masters, the British Open, and the PGA Championship.

What was the first publicly televised sporting event?

It was a Japanese baseball game, broadcast on September 27, 1931. The Ushigome and Awazi Shichiku

Higher Elementary Schools battled it out on the Tozuka Baseball Ground, watched by viewers on 8-by-5-inch screens.

Where was the first All-Star baseball game played?
On July 6, 1933, in Comiskey Park, Chicago, home of the White Sox. The American League won, 4–2.

Where was the first night baseball game played?
At Crosley Field in Cincinnati on May 24, 1935—a game between the Cincinnati Reds and Philadelphia Phillies. The Reds beat the Phillies, 2–1.

Who were the first players inducted into the Baseball Hall of Fame?
The first group, inducted in 1936, consisted of Ty Cobb, Walter Johnson, Christy Mathewson, Babe Ruth, and Honus Wagner. Tyrus Raymond Cobb (1886–1961), "the Georgia Peach," had played for the Detroit Tigers. Walter Perry Johnson (1887–1946) had pitched for the Washington Senators. Christopher Mathewson (1880–1925) had been a pitcher for the New York Giants. George Herman ("Babe") Ruth (1895–1948) was the New York Yankees' "Sultan of Swat." John Peter ("Honus") Wagner (1867–1955), "the Flying Dutchman," was a shortstop for the Pittsburgh Pirates.

Which female figure skater has won the greatest number of Olympic gold medals?
Sonja Henie (1912–1969) of Norway, who won the gold medal in 1928, 1932, and 1936. Between 1927

and 1936, she also won 10 world figure-skating championships.

Which baseball player holds the record for stealing home?

Ty Cobb stole home 46 times during his 22-year career with the Detroit Tigers.

Who was the first man to win the tennis grand slam in the same calendar year?

J. Donald (Don) Budge (b. 1915) in 1938.

How many consecutive games did Lou Gehrig appear in?

From 1925 to 1939, the Yankee first baseman appeared in 2,130 consecutive games—an unmatched record.

Has any jockey ever won the Triple Crown more than once?

Eddie ("Banana Nose") Arcaro won it twice—in 1941 on Whirlaway and in 1948 on Citation.

What teams constitute the Big Ten?

The football conference that became the Big Ten, or the Western Conference, was formed in 1896 by the Universities of Chicago, Illinois, Michigan, Minnesota, and Wisconsin, along with Northwestern and Purdue universities. Iowa and Indiana joined in 1899 and Ohio State in 1912. The University of Chicago dropped out in 1946 after terminating its football program. The conference was really "the Big Nine" until Michigan State joined in 1949. In December 1989, it was announced that Penn State University would become the 11th member, though the conference did not plan to change its name to "the Big Eleven."

When did baseball's New York Giants become the San Francisco Giants?

The team moved to San Francisco for the start of the 1958 season. The final game of the New York Giants at New York's Polo Grounds was played against the Pittsburgh Pirates.

When did the Brooklyn Dodgers move to Los Angeles?

They left Ebbets Field after the 1957 baseball season.

Was Wilt Chamberlain the first pro basketball player over seven feet tall?

Although he was not the first seven-foot-tall basketball player, he was the first to dispel the then common notion that big, tall men were awkward players. At 7 feet, 1 inch and 275 pounds, he signed with the Philadelphia Warriors on May 30, 1959. He scored 43 points and got 28 rebounds in his debut game against the New York Knicks. His record-setting performances raised the demand for tall players and started the "Seven-Foot Revolution."

What is the highest-scoring pro basketball game to date?
A 1983 game in which the Detroit Pistons beat the Denver Nuggets, 186–183.

What was Jack Nicklaus's first major golf tournament win?
The 1962 U.S. Open, where he beat the popular champion Arnold Palmer. It was Nicklaus's second year as a pro. He went on to win 71 tour victories and 20 major championships over the next two decades.

What was the longest golf drive in PGA history?
The official PGA record is 406 yards by Jack L. Hamm on July 12, 1986.

When was the first Superbowl held?
It was held in 1967 between the Green Bay Packers and the Kansas City Chiefs. The Packers won, 35–10.

Which hockey player holds the lifetime record for scoring goals?
Gordie Howe of the Detroit Red Wings, who scored 801 goals in his 25-year career, from 1946 to 1971.

What is the longest pro football game on record?
The game on December 25, 1971, between the Miami Dolphins and the Kansas City Chiefs lasted 82 minutes and 40 seconds. It went into a second period of sudden

death before Garo Yepremian kicked a field goal and won the game for the Dolphins, 27–24.

What type of tennis stroke did Chris Evert popularize?

Chris Evert popularized the two-fisted backhand, which she began using out of necessity when she was six years old. Beginning her professional career in 1972, Evert has won close to 150 women's singles titles and more than 1,000 career matches.

How long was Secretariat's career?

Secretariat raced for only 16 months in 1972 and 1973. In that time the chestnut stallion became the first horse in 25 years to win the Triple Crown, set record times in the Kentucky Derby and the Belmont Stakes, and won 16 of his 31 races. He was retired to stud in November 1973 because his owner needed the $6.08 million in breeding shares. Secretariat died at the age of 19 in 1989, survived by more than 300 offspring.

What is the longest baseball game on record?

A game running eight hours and six minutes was played by the Chicago White Sox and the Milwaukee Brewers on May 9, 1984. The White Sox won, 7–6.

Who was pitching when Hank Aaron hit his 715th career home run?

Los Angeles Dodger Al Downing was the pitcher who watched as the ball flew over the left-field fence of Atlanta Stadium on April 8, 1974. Atlanta Brave Henry

Louis Aaron had broken the long-standing record for career home runs set by Babe Ruth in the 1930s.

How long does it take to walk around the world?
It took David Kunst a little over four years—from June 10, 1970, to October 5, 1974. One other man—George Schilling—claimed in an unconfirmed report to have accomplished the feat between June 1897 and June 1904.

Where was Martina Navratilova born?
She was born in Prague, Czechoslovakia, on October 18, 1956, as Martina Subertova. When her mother later divorced and remarried, Martina took the name of her stepfather, Miroslav Navratil, adding the traditional feminine ending *ova*.

> *When did she come to the United States?*
> She defected in September 1975 during the U.S. Open.

Who was the first pro athlete indicted for a crime committed during play?
Dave Forbes of the Boston Bruins hockey team. He was alleged to have used aggressive force on an opponent. On July 18, 1975, his trial for criminal assault ended in a hung jury.

How many times did Muhammad Ali battle for the heavyweight boxing title?
He defended it 19 times—5 times in 1966 alone, 4 in 1976. But he doesn't hold a candle to Joe Louis, who defended his title 25 times, with 7 fights in 1941.

What is the fastest speed for a male skier? Female?
The fastest downhill speed to date for a man is 139.03 miles per hour by Michael Pruffer of France. The fastest woman on skis is Tara Mulari of Finland, clocked at 133.234 miles per hour. Both records were set at Les Arcs, France, in 1988.

How many ways can a batter reach first base without hitting the ball?
There are six ways: a walk; being hit by a pitch; a dropped third strike; catcher's interference; a pitched or thrown ball intended to catch a runner that "goes into a stand or a bench, or over or through a field fence or backstop" (rule 705[h]); and when, on a ball four or strike three, a pitch "passes the catcher and lodges in the umpire's mask or paraphernalia" (rule 705[i]).

How much does an official baseball weigh?
Between 5 and 5.25 ounces.

How wide is a golf hole? How deep is it?
It is 4.25 inches in diameter and at least 4 inches deep.

How high is the regulation basketball hoop?
It is 10 feet above the floor.

How many players do you need to start a polo game?
You need two teams with four players each and horses for all of them. The aim is to drive a wooden ball down a grass field and between two goalposts.

New baseball gloves are supposed to be broken in with neat's-foot oil. What is it?

Neat is a now obsolete term for cattle. Neat's-foot oil is the oil extracted from the hooves and slim bones of oxen or cattle. In olden days, the oil was also used as medicine and as shoe polish.

How big is a hockey puck?

Usually made of vulcanized rubber, it is 3 inches in diameter, 1 inch thick, and weighs 5.5 to 6 ounces.

What sports personality said, "The opera ain't over 'til the fat lady sings"?

It was *not* Yogi Berra. Former Washington Bullets coach Dick Motta popularized the saying during the 1978 NBA playoffs, but it was Dan Cook, a television sports announcer and writer for the *San Antonio Express-News*, who invented it.

TRADEMARKS

•••••

Who invented Tupperware?

An inventor from Massachusetts named Earl D. Tupper in 1942. In the 1930s, Tupper, a chemist at Du Pont, experimented with a new durable plastic called polyethylene. Tupper thought it could be used for all types of housewares, and he developed some test products. The first piece of Tupperware, a bathroom cup, was introduced to department stores in 1945. It outsold its competitors. Tupperware's sales mushroomed when Tupper created the marketing device of the home party. By 1954, in-home sales topped $25 million.

Why does Ivory soap float?

Too much air—originally an error in production. In 1878, Harley Procter and cousin James Gamble decided to create for their company a white soap that would rival the popular castile soaps of their competitors. The product was successful. Then, in 1879, a worker mistakenly allowed the soap solution to be overmixed. The new version of the soap was an immediate success because it bobbed to the surface of the water.

How did Shell Oil get its name?

The company that eventually bore the name Shell Oil Company was originally a novelty shop in London called The Shell Shop. In the mid-1800s, shop owner Marcus Samuel became successful selling boxes of pretty seashells. Imported shells also brought in money, and his international trade business really expanded when he found he could also export kerosene. The Shell Shop became Shell Transport and Trading Company—and eventually Shell Oil Company.

When was denim first used to make Levi's jeans?

Originally San Francisco tailor Levi Strauss made jeans from canvas. But in the early 1860s, he started using a softer fabric imported from Nîmes, France. Known in French as *serge de Nîmes*, the material was called denim in the United States.

How does a log cabin figure in the naming of Log Cabin syrup?

At the time, in 1887, the lowly cabin was meant to evoke thoughts of an all-American hero—Abraham Lincoln—and thus increase sales. Grocer P. J. Towle, creator of the syrup, a blend of sugar cane with Vermont and Canadian maple sugars, had rejected the idea of naming his creation Abraham Lincoln syrup. But the log cabin idea worked—and in fact determined the shape for the syrup's tin container until World War II, when tin was needed for the war effort.

How many peanuts are in each box of Cracker Jack?

There are nine nuts per ounce, a smaller proportion than in the original 1893 box. But there is a prize, and that didn't become part of the package until 1913.

Was there an Aunt Jemima?

There was a woman who acted as Aunt Jemima— Nancy Green, of Montgomery County, Kentucky. This cook for a judge's family in Chicago was lured by executives of the Davis Milling Company to promote the pancake mix at Chicago's World's Columbian Exposition in 1893. She had served 1 million pancakes by the time the fair was over.

Is there any connection between the Avon Lady and Shakespeare's hometown, Stratford-upon-Avon?

Yes. In 1896 in New York City, D. H. McConnell abandoned door-to-door bookselling and formed the California Perfume Company, which marketed scents the same way. His company expanded and McConnell built a factory in Suffern, New York. On the 50th anniversary of the company, McConnell changed its name. He chose Avon because he admired Shakespeare.

Who is the "Tootsie" of Tootsie Rolls?

It is Clara Hirschfield, the daughter of the candy's creator, Leo Hirschfield, who had given her this pet name. He gave the name to the candy as well, which entered the American market in 1896.

How was the car known as the Fiat named?

The word *fiat* means an authoritative decree (from the Latin for "let it be done"). But the Italian car company founded in Turin in 1899 adopted its name as an acronym for Fabbrica Italiana Automobili Torino (Italian Motorcar Works, Turin).

What does the name Kodak stand for?

According to George Eastman, founder of Eastman Kodak, the name is his invention: "I knew a trade name must be short, vigorous, incapable of being misspelled . . . and in order to satisfy trademark laws, it must mean nothing. . . . The letter *k* had been a favorite with me— it seemed a strong, incisive sort of letter. . . . Then it became a question of trying out a great number of combinations of letters that made words starting and ending with *k*." The name Kodak is the result.

What does the name Sanka stand for?

This 1903 creation is a contraction of the French phrase *sans caféine*. The first decaffeinated coffee arrived in America by accident that year: A shipload of coffee coming from Europe to coffee importer Dr. Ludwig Roselius became waterlogged—and thus decaffeinated.

How did Maxwell House coffee get to be "good to the last drop"?

The phrase belongs to President Theodore Roosevelt, who, while visiting Andrew Jackson's home, the Hermitage, in Nashville, Tennessee, drank a cup of Maxwell House coffee and was offered a refill. He is said to have replied, "Will I have another? Delighted! It's good to the last drop!" By the way, there actually was a Maxwell House. A luxury hotel in Nashville, Maxwell House was the place where, in the 1880s, the coffee was first served.

Who was the first Fuller Brush man?

Alfred Carl Fuller came to the United States from Norway in 1903, and after working at a variety of jobs, he began selling brushes door-to-door in 1905. By 1910, he had a staff of 25 salesmen. Over the years, Fuller adapted by expanding his line to include a variety of household cleaning products. When he retired in 1943, annual sales topped $10 million. In 1948, Red Skelton starred in the movie *The Fuller Brush Man*; in 1950, Lucille Ball did the same in *The Fuller Brush Girl*. In the 1990s, the Fuller Brush man may be no more, but the company lives on. Headquartered in North Carolina, it still thrives, primarily through catalog orders.

Was there a camel that became the Camel cigarette's trademark?

The original camel was an Arabian dromedary named "Old Joe" that appeared in the Barnum & Bailey Circus at the turn of the century. At that time, the R. J. Reynolds Tobacco Company was looking for an exotic name and concept to link with its new Oriental and Turkish blend cigarette. On October 21, 1913, Camel cigarettes were launched, with the now famous illustration of Old Joe on its wrapper.

How was Noxzema named?

Developed in 1914 by George Bunting, a Baltimore pharmacist, the skin cream was originally called Dr. Bunting's Sunburn Remedy. He searched in vain for a better name until one day a customer entered his drugstore and told him, "Your sunburn cream sure knocked out my eczema." The concoction that "knocks eczema" became Noxzema.

For what is the Dixie Cup named?

Developed between 1908 and 1912 by Hugh Moore as the healthful "individual drinking cup" for public water sources, it was originally called the Health Kup. It did not catch on until inventor Moore gave it a new name. The producer of the cups was the Dixie Doll Company, which reminded Moore of a New Orleans bank that issued its own money, mainly $10 bills, or "Dixies." Thus, in 1919, the Dixie Cup was born.

Who invented the Band-Aid?

Robert Johnson, a pharmacist from Brooklyn, New York, and partner in a Brooklyn pharmaceutical supply firm, believed that individually sealed sterile bandages could drastically reduce the rate of hospital infections, which in some cases ran to 90 percent. By the mid-1800s, he and his brothers formed a pharmaceutical company that produced and sold the bandages to hospitals. In 1920, a company employee, Earle Dickson, devised small sterile bandages for his wife's minor injuries. Band-Aids eventually became the standard for do-it-yourself dressings.

Was there a Dr. Scholl?

Yes. In the late nineteenth century, William ("Billy") Scholl left farm life in La Porte, Indiana, for life as a shoemaker in Chicago. After noticing how much abuse the average foot takes, he decided to become a podiatrist and treat the problems he saw. Once established as a medical doctor, he created foot products such as the Foot Eazer, an arch support. Eventually he opened factories in the United States and Canada to manufacture the many products that bore his name.

Is the portrait of the Gerber baby really a painting of the young Humphrey Bogart?

No. The now famous portrait was of a baby girl named Ann Turner and was sketched by artist Dorothy Hope Smith in 1928.

In men's underwear, what does BVD stand for?

Not, as once believed, "Baby's Ventilated Diapers" or "Boys' Ventilated Drawers," but the three founders of the company—Bradley, Voorhees, and Day.

Who invented Alka-Seltzer?

The idea came from a newspaper editor in Elkhart, Indiana, in the 1920s and was brought to the public by Hub Beardsley, president of the Dr. Miles Laboratories (now Miles Laboratories). Beardsley learned that an entire newspaper staff had remained free of influenza during an epidemic when they took the editor's prescription of aspirin and baking soda. Beardsley knew he had found a money-making product. Launched in 1931, the tablet was a nationwide success before the end of the decade.

Why does MGM have a lion?

The lion, developed before the formation of MGM, was the original trademark for the newly formed (Samuel) Goldwyn Pictures Corporation. It was the creation of a young advertising man named Howard Dietz, who was inspired by his alma mater Columbia University's football song, "Roar, Lion, Roar!" Later on, Dietz also came up with the motto *Ars Gratia Artis*—"Art for Art's Sake." In 1924, when Goldwyn Pictures merged with the Metro Studio and Louis B. Mayer to form MGM, the trademark animal—now named Leo— went along. Leo made his first on-screen roar at New York City's Astor Theater on July 31, 1928, at the premiere of *White Shadows in the South Seas*.

Was the Baby Ruth candy bar named for the base-ball player?

No, it was named for Ruth Cleveland, the oldest daughter of President Grover Cleveland.

How did Chanel N°5 get its name?

It is not because it was the fifth formulation of the mixture. Coco Chanel considered five a lucky number, and when she introduced the perfume in 1921, she did so on the fifth day of May, the fifth month. She called the fragrance Chanel N°5.

Who created the Burma-Shave signs that ran up and down American roadways earlier in this century?

The now legendary and defunct advertisements were developed in 1926 by Allan Odell, the son of the founder of the Burma-Vita Company. Burma-Shave was a new product—the first brushless shaving cream—and in the 1920s it was difficult to sell. But when Odell saw a series of roadside signs for a filling station, he decided to transfer the idea to his product. The first six signs, spaced 100 feet apart, appeared on U.S. Highway 65 near Lakewell, Minnesota, in September 1926 and read: Chin Up / Face / The War / Is / Over. By the 1960s, over 7,000 sets of signs were seen across the country, with jingles provided by national contests. Odell's favorite was:

> *Within this vale*
> *Of toil and sin*
> *Your head grows bald*
> *But not your chin.*

How did 7UP get its name?

The *7* stands for the soft drink's original 7-ounce bottle, the *UP* for the bubbles from its carbonation. In

1929, when the drink was first introduced by Saint Louis businessman Charles L. Grigg, it was called Bib-Label Lithiated Lemon-Lime Soda. The name was derived from one of its original ingredients, lithium salts.

Why did bottles of Dr. Pepper bear the numbers 10, 2, and 4?

They represented the times between meals when a person's energy is at its lowest and can be revived by Dr. Pepper.

Is the Bic pen named for someone named Bic?

It is named for Baron Biche. But Biche did not invent the ballpoint pen—Hungarian László Biró did, in 1938. Biche's French firm, Bic, took over the English company that had agreed to produce the pens. In England the pen is still known as a "biro," in France as a "bic."

What does M&M stand for?

For Mars and Merrie—Victor Mars and his associate Mr. Merrie, who developed the candy in 1941.

How many candies of each color go into the average bag of M&M's?

Following consumer testing, M&M/Mars decided upon the following breakdown for plain M&M's:

Brown. 30 percent
Red. 20 percent
Yellow. 20 percent

Green. 10 percent
Orange. 10 percent
Tan. 10 percent

For peanut M&M's, it is:

Brown. 30 percent
Red. 20 percent
Yellow. 20 percent
Green. 20 percent
Orange. 10 percent

What does the *K* in K rations stand for?

Most likely, it represents the first letter of the last name of the product's developer, Ancel Keys (b. 1904). Keys, a physiologist from Minnesota, developed the portions of food for soldiers in World War II.

What is L.S./M.F.T.?

It means Lucky Strike Means Fine Tobacco and was the creation of George Washington Hill, son of Buck Duke, founder of the American Tobacco Company. The slogan, introduced in the early 1940s, became so popular that by 1944 its acronym—L.S./M.F.T.—was printed on the bottom of every Lucky Strike package.

What is Silly Putty made of?

This rubberlike compound is composed, in part, of boric acid and silicone oil. Invented at the General Electric laboratories in the 1940s as an inexpensive synthetic rubber for use during World War II, it gained its greatest popularity when New Haven, Connecticut, store owner Paul Hodgson bought a large quantity of it, put it in small plastic eggs, and called it Silly Putty.

Who was the Man in the Hathaway Shirt?

Baron George Wrangell, descendant of Russian and Italian royalty, was working as an artist's model before advertising executive David Ogilvy chose him for the Hathaway advertisements in the late 1940s. The eye-patch (cost: 50 cents) was Ogilvy's idea.

What is the name of the Michelin Man?

The fat little man made of Michelin tires is named Bibendum. He can be seen on the covers of all Michelin travel guides.

Who invented Pac-Man?

It was twenty-seven-year-old Turn Iwatani, who worked for Namco Limited of Japan, a producer of video games and computer software.

Who invented the teaser of the 1980s—Rubik's Cube?

The 27 subcubes that rotate on horizontal and vertical axes were designed by and named for Erno Rubik, a teacher of architecture and design at the School for Commercial Artists in Budapest.

What does *Frusen Glädjé* mean?

It means "frozen delight" in Swedish.

What does Häagen-Dazs *mean?*
It has no particular meaning. It is a name created by its developer, Reuben Mattus, a Polish emigré living in the United States, to convey a European sensibility.

How much beef does McDonald's use each year?
Assuming that the average hamburger weighs 3 ounces (actually 1.6 ounces for the hamburger, 4 ounces for the quarter-pounder) and that the average quantity sold annually is 3 billion burgers, McDonald's uses about 560 million pounds of hamburger each year.

• 23 •

U.S. PRESIDENTS

◆◆◆◆◆

In order, which five persons are in line of succession to the presidency?

1. Vice-President
2. Speaker of the House of Representatives
3. President Pro Tempore of the Senate
4. Secretary of State
5. Secretary of the Treasury

How much money did George Washington borrow to go to his inauguration?
In 1789, George Washington was wealthy in land but short of cash. He borrowed £600 to travel from Mount Vernon to New York City, the site of his first inauguration.

Where was the first U.S. presidential mansion?
The first presidential mansion was located at One Cherry Street in New York City. It was *not* called the

White House. George Washington lived there from April 23, 1789, to February 23, 1790.

Was Lincoln the first president born in a log cabin?
No, Andrew Jackson holds that honor. He was born on March 15, 1767, in a log cabin in Waxhaw, South Carolina. He was also the first president born in South Carolina and the first born west of the Allegheny Mountains.

Which signers of the Declaration of Independence later became presidents? Which future presidents signed the Constitution?
Only two future presidents signed the Declaration of Independence—John Adams and Thomas Jefferson. George Washington and James Madison were the only two to sign the Constitution.

Who was the first president defeated for reelection?
John Adams (1735–1826), the second president, in 1801. Thomas Jefferson defeated him and served two terms, from 1801 to 1809.

Who was the first president born after the United States declared its independence?
The eighth president, Martin Van Buren (1836–1844), was born on December 5, 1782.

Who was the first Speaker of the House to be elected president?
James K. Polk, who served as Speaker of the House from 1835 to 1839, was sworn in as president in 1845. He served one term, leaving office in 1849.

Which U.S. presidents were bachelors?

James Buchanan (1857–1861) was the only lifelong bachelor. He had been engaged in 1819 to Ann Caroline Coleman, but she died of an overdose of laudanum before the two were married.

What play was Lincoln viewing at Ford's Theater when he was assassinated?

He was watching *Our American Cousin*, by Tom Taylor, on the evening of April 14, 1865, when John Wilkes Booth entered Lincoln's private box and fired his one-shot derringer. Lincoln's bodyguard had stepped away for a drink of water.

Who was the first president born west of the Mississippi?

It was Herbert Hoover, born on August 10, 1874, in West Branch, Iowa.

What was Gerald R. Ford's real name?

He was born Leslie Lynch King, Jr., in 1913. His parents divorced when he was an infant; his mother then married Gerald R. Ford, Sr., who adopted the future president and gave him his name.

Who was president when the federal income tax went into effect?

It was 24th president William Howard Taft (1857–1930) who was in office when the 16th Amendment to the Constitution—which gave the federal government power to collect tax "among the several states and without regard to census"—was passed in 1909 and ratified in 1913.

Who was the first president holding a doctorate?

It was Woodrow Wilson (1856–1924), the 28th president. He received a doctorate from Johns Hopkins University in 1886; his thesis was entitled "Congressional Government, a Study in American Politics."

Why did President Woodrow Wilson keep sheep at the White House?

The sheep were part of the war effort. In 1917, during World War I, President Wilson arranged for a small flock of sheep to graze on the White House lawn, thus freeing up the regular gardeners for military service. Although the sheep began eating more of the White House grounds than the lawn, the Wilsons continued to defend them—citing, among other things, the vast amounts of "White House wool" the sheep generated for the Red Cross.

When was Franklin D. Roosevelt stricken with polio?

In August 1921, when he was 39. By that time, he had been assistant secretary of the navy, a vice presidential nominee (in 1920), and a member of the New York State Senate.

Where was Teapot Dome, source of the 1920s presidential scandal?

The government-owned land, rich in oil, was located in Wyoming. The scandal began when a Senate investigating committee discovered that the Teapot Dome and Elk Hills, California, reserves had been secretly leased by Secretary of the Interior Albert B. Fall to private oil companies in 1922. Fall was eventually convicted of bribery and the entire Harding administration was tarnished.

What are the presidents carved on Mount Rushmore, South Dakota, meant to represent?

The four 60-foot-high likenesses, sculpted between 1925 and 1941, are meant to represent the following: George Washington, the nation's founding; Thomas Jefferson, its political philosophy; Abraham Lincoln, its preservation; and Theodore Roosevelt, its expansion and conservation.

Who changed the name of the Maryland presidential retreat from Shangri-La to Camp David?

Dwight D. Eisenhower changed it in 1953, naming it after his grandson.

What is the shortest term of office of any president?

William Henry Harrison died in 1841 after only 31 days in office. James A. Garfield was a close second: In 1881, he died of a gunshot wound after only six months in office.

How many U.S. presidents have been assassinated?

Four: Abraham Lincoln in 1865, James A. Garfield in 1881, William McKinley in 1901, and John F. Kennedy in 1963.

What is the origin of the quote used in President John F. Kennedy's inaugural speech, "Ask not what your country can do for you; ask what you can do for your country"?

Another form of the quote was spoken by the young Kennedy's headmaster at Choate, a prep school in Wallingford, Connecticut. The headmaster told his students, "Ask not what your school can do for you; ask what you can do for your school"; and Kennedy adapted the phrase.

How many times did Harold Stassen run for the presidency?

Three, though it seems like more. Born in 1907, Harold Edward Stassen, governor of Minnesota from 1938 to 1945, tried unsuccessfully to win the Republican nomination in 1948, 1964, and 1968. He has gone on trying in the comedy routines of others ever since.

How many articles of impeachment did the House Judiciary Committee recommend before President Nixon resigned?

There were three before his resignation on August 8, 1974. Twenty-eight minutes after Nixon delivered his letter of resignation, Gerald R. Ford was sworn in as the new president.

Was Gerald R. Ford the first incumbent president to agree to public debates with a challenger?

Yes. He gained that claim to fame in 1976 when he debated Jimmy Carter. The debates helped Ford to narrow Carter's lead in the race, although he eventually lost the election.

How would the president "push the button" for a nuclear attack?

As depicted in some spy movies, the president would not press a button; he would make a phone call. To begin a nuclear attack, the president telephones the commander in chief at the Strategic Air Command in Omaha, Nebraska; several officers at SAC would verify the president's orders. Once verified, instructions would go to bomber and missile crews, who would enact a series of movements to arm the bombs.

Which U.S. state has been the birthplace of the most presidents?

Virginia has the honor, with eight: Washington, Jefferson, Madison, Monroe, William Henry Harrison, Tyler, Taylor, and Wilson. Ohio is second, with seven: Grant, Hayes, Garfield, Benjamin Harrison, McKinley, Taft, and Harding.

Which vice presidents have been elected president—besides those who first gained the office when their predecessors died or resigned?

John Adams, Thomas Jefferson, Martin Van Buren, Richard M. Nixon, and George Bush.

What are the executive departments represented in the president's cabinet?

In alphabetical order, they are: Agriculture, Commerce, Defense, Education, Energy, Health and Human Services, Housing and Urban Development, Interior, Justice, Labor, State, Transportation, Treasury, and Veterans Affairs.

How many presidents served in the armed forces?
Twenty-two of 41. They were:

George Washington
James Monroe
Andrew Jackson
William Henry Harrison
Zachary Taylor
James Buchanan
Abraham Lincoln
Andrew Johnson
Ulysses S. Grant
Rutherford B. Hayes
James A. Garfield
Benjamin Harrison
William McKinley
Theodore Roosevelt
Harry Truman
Dwight D. Eisenhower
John F. Kennedy
Richard M. Nixon
Gerald R. Ford
Jimmy Carter
Ronald Reagan
George Bush

How many U.S. state capitals are named after presidents?

Four: Jackson, Mississippi; Jefferson City, Missouri; Lincoln, Nebraska; and Madison, Wisconsin.

What were the names of the following presidents' dogs?

George Washington. Captain, Cloe, Forester, Lady, Mopsey, Rover, Taster, Tipler, etc.
Abraham Lincoln. Jip
Franklin D. Roosevelt. Fala and Tiny
John F. Kennedy. Charley, Shannon, and Wolf

• 24 •

WHO WAS WHO

♦♦♦♦♦

Did Pythagoras discover the Pythagorean theorem?
Since the ancient Greek mathematician and philosopher (fifth century B.C.) left no writings behind, it is hard to tell. His disciples in the Pythagorean school credited him with the theorem concerning the relative lengths of the sides of a right triangle, but it was probably developed later, when mathematical concepts had reached a more advanced state.

What happened to Pontius Pilate after he ordered the crucifixion of Christ?
He killed himself. In A.D. 36, Caligula ordered Pilate to Rome to answer charges of cruelty in the massacre of a group of Samaritans. Shortly thereafter, Pilate committed suicide, possibly by order of Caligula or in anticipation of harsh treatment.

What is Pliny the Elder's claim to fame? Pliny the Younger's?

Pliny the Elder (A.D. 23–79) was an encyclopedist whose reputation as an expert on scientific matters endured until the Middle Ages. His adopted son, Pliny the Younger (c. A.D. 61–c. A.D. 113), was a lawyer and administrator known mainly for the large collection of private letters he left behind.

Have any world leaders ever died while having sex?

At least three have: Attila the Hun (c. 406–453), French president Félix Faure (1841–1899), and Pope Leo VIII (d. 965). Catherine the Great did not.

Who was the original Peeping Tom?

He was a tailor who dared to look at Lady Godiva as she rode through Coventry. In 1040, Lady Godiva's husband, Leofric, Earl of Mercia and Lord of Coventry, agreed to rescind a tax on the town if Lady Godiva rode naked through the streets. Godiva asked everyone to observe custody of the eyes—and everyone did, except Tom.

Who was the Hobson behind a Hobson's choice?

A Hobson's choice is a situation that forces a person to accept whatever is offered or go without. The phrase was inspired by sixteenth-century entrepreneur Thomas Hobson, who hired out horses in strict rotation at Cambridge University. There was no choosing by the customer—it was strictly Hobson's choice.

In addition to his many other predictions, is it true that Nostradamus foresaw his own death?

Michel de Notredame, aka Nostradamus (1503–1566), seems to have done so. On July 1, 1566, his assistant rose to leave him for the evening, saying, "Tomorrow, master," to which Nostradamus said, "Tomorrow at sunrise, I shall no longer be here." The next morning he was found dead from an attack of dropsy.

Who built the Taj Mahal?

It was built between 1632 and 1650 in Agra, India, by Shah Jahan as a tomb for his wife. The marble structure is considered a superb representation of the Mogul style.

Was there an original Goody Two-Shoes?

As the subject of the first children's book of the same name, this character helped to usher in the children's book industry. Goody Two-Shoes was a poor girl, who, when given a pair of shoes, became so happy that she told everyone she met about them. The tale was written by Oliver Goldsmith in 1765.

Who is the Mason-Dixon line named for?

The two men who laid the line gave it its name. Charles Mason and Jeremiah Dixon laid the line sometime between 1763 and 1767 at 39°43'26" north latitude. Originally it was the boundary between Maryland and Pennsylvania. Later it marked the line between slave states and free states.

What was Sojourner Truth's real name?

She was born a slave named Isabella in 1797. After escaping to freedom in 1843, she became the first black female orator to speak out against slavery—traveling the North on foot to spread her message. She died in 1883.

Who was the first chauvinist?

The term *chauvinism* originally referred to Nicolas Chauvin, a French soldier of the Napoleonic era whose devotion to Napoleon was considered excessive and unreasonable. He later appeared in a number of plays and literary works, including Baroness Orczy's *Scarlet Pimpernel* (1905), always representing an exaggerated patriotism. The term has since taken on a more general meaning of smug superiority.

Who was the McGuffey who gave us the *McGuffey Eclectic Readers*?

An American college teacher and political conservative, William Holmes McGuffey (1800–1873) wrote his first readers in 1836, following with more in the next two decades. The schoolbooks have sold 122 million copies.

Who founded the Pinkerton Detective Agency?

Allan Pinkerton (1819–1884), a Scotsman who moved to Chicago in 1842. He was deputy sheriff of Cook County before resigning in 1850 to open the Pinkerton National Detective Agency, specializing at first in railway theft cases. The agency's motto was We Never Sleep, printed under an open eye.

Who is the most married person in history?

Mongkut of Siam—the king in *The King and I*—had 9,000 wives and concubines. Solomon, by contrast, had only 700.

Has a woman ever won the U.S. Medal of Honor?

There has been only one female winner—Mary Walker, who served as a surgeon in the 52nd Ohio Regiment during the Civil War. She was awarded the medal in 1865 by President Andrew Johnson.

How tall was Tom Thumb?

Charles Sherwood Stratton (1838–1883)—the star of P. T. Barnum's circus and better known as General Tom Thumb—was 3 feet, 4 inches tall when he died.

Who was the tallest person ever recorded?

Robert Pershing Wadlow (1919–1940). Born in Alton, Illinois, Wadlow was 8 feet, 11.1 inches tall when he died.

Who is known as "the man who ate Democrats"?

It was Alfred Packer (1842–1907), who in 1873 guided a party of 20 men into the San Juan Mountains, continued in heavy snows against advice, and returned alone, saying his companions had abandoned him. Months afterward, search parties discovered the bodies of the missing men, most stripped of flesh. Packer was tried, found guilty of murder, and sentenced to 40 years of hard labor. Before he left the courtroom, he was assured of a place in posterity when the judge told him sternly, "Packer, you depraved Republican son of a bitch, there were only five Democrats in Hinsdale County, and you ate them all!"

Who were the people behind the names of the following concoctions?

> *Gimlet.* Sir T. O. Gimlette, a British naval surgeon who in 1890 developed the drink as a healthful cocktail.
> *Grand Marnier.* Named (in jest?) by hotel owner César Ritz for a short businessman named Marnier Lapostolle, the inventor of the liqueur.
> *Mickey Finn.* A turn-of-the-century Chicago bartender who served the spiked drink to clients he planned to rob.
> *Tom Collins.* A London bartender of the 1800s who worked at Limmer's Old House.
> *Harvey Wallbanger.* Named for California surfer Tom Harvey (c. 1970), who would bang into walls after drinking this cocktail.

What was Geronimo's real name?

The Apache leader (1829–1908) was known to his tribe as Goyathlay, meaning "One Who Yawns." The nickname Geronimo is probably a corruption of the Spanish name Jerónimo.

How long did it take Stanley to find Livingstone?

Henry Morton Stanley, a journalist, was commissioned by the *New York Herald* in 1871 to find the explorer David Livingstone, who had been missing for two years. Stanley trekked through Africa for six months before meeting Livingstone, the only other white man within 1,000 miles.

Was there a Typhoid Mary?

Yes, her name was Mary Mallon (1870–1938). She was an institutional and household cook who spread the disease from house to house in the New York City area in the early twentieth century.

Whom did Theodore Roosevelt call a "filthy little atheist"?

Thomas Paine, the eighteenth-century American pamphleteer who wrote *Common Sense*. Paine was actually 5 feet, 10 inches tall, neat in appearance, and believed in God.

Who was the Girl in the Red Velvet Swing?

She was Evelyn Nesbit Thaw, a beautiful young woman who had been seduced at age fifteen by architect Stanford White. At the time of the seduction, she was single and a showgirl in the "Floradora" company. She met White in a room with a red velvet swing. After she married, her husband Harry Thaw grew enraged at the liaison and killed White on June 28, 1906. The murder occurred on the roof of one of the buildings White had designed, the second Madison Square Garden.

What was the name of the black explorer who accompanied Admiral Robert E. Peary to the North Pole?

Matthew A. Henson (1866–1955), who had worked with Peary since an 1887 expedition in Nicaragua. Henson and Peary were the only two of a team of six explorers to reach what Peary claimed was the North Pole on April 7, 1909.

What was Mata Hari's birth name? Was she ever caught by the authorities?

Fleeing from Holland in the early 1900s, a Dutch officer's wife named Margaretha Geertruida Zelle changed her name to Mata Hari. At first she became a licentious dancer and later the most notorious spy of World War I. Arrested in her Paris hotel in February 1917, she was shot by a firing squad on October 15 of that year. As the squad raised its rifles, she is said to have smiled and winked.

After all his narrow escapes, what finally caused Harry Houdini's death?

Acute appendicitis overcame the former Erich Weiss on October 31, 1926—Halloween. He was 52 years old.

Who was the It Girl?

Silent screen siren Clara Bow (1905–1965) picked up the nickname after starring as a flapper in *It* in 1927.

Who was the It Boy?
Gary Cooper was briefly called by this moniker when he began dating Ms. Bow. He is said to have ended the relationship in order to get rid of the nickname.

Who was Balto the Wonder Dog?

The dog—memorialized in a bas-relief in New York's Central Park and celebrated in dozens of Johnny Carson's skits—actually existed and was a hero in his day. Balto led a dog-sled expedition through 600 miles of Arctic terrain to deliver an antitoxin needed to save the residents of Nome, Alaska, during a 1925 diphtheria epidemic. The driver of the seven-husky team was blinded by snow and had to place all trust in Balto. Balto completed his mission but died upon his arrival in Nome.

Who was the head of the Vichy government in France during World War II? What became of him?

Henri Philippe Pétain (1856–1951) was a military hero in World War I and premier of France in 1940. In June of that year, he called for an armistice with Germany and became the "chief of state" of the puppet government at Vichy. After the war, he was sentenced to death, but the sentence was commuted to life imprisonment. He died at the age of 95 in a military prison on an island off the coast of France.

Who was Tokyo Rose?

She was a Japanese–American named Iva d'Aquino (b. 1916) known for her World War II radio broadcasts aimed at weakening the morale of U.S. servicemen. Convicted of treason after the war, she received a presidential pardon in 1977.

Who was her European counterpart?
She had several, all known as Axis Sally and all broadcasting to GIs in Europe. The most famous Axis Sallys were Mildred Elizabeth Sisk and Rita Louise Zucca.

For whom is Chicago's O'Hare Field named?
The airport is named for Edward Henry O'Hare, a U.S. aviator who shot down five Japanese planes on November 27, 1943, and is credited with saving the U.S. aircraft carrier *Lexington*. He died in the air battle.

Which was insured for the most money—Fred Astaire's feet, Betty Grable's legs, or Jimmy Durante's nose?
Astaire's feet, insured for $650,000, were at the top of this list. Grable's legs were insured for only $250,000, Durante's nose for $140,000.

What was Lady Bird Johnson's real name?
Claudia Alta Taylor Johnson (b. 1912). The wife of President Lyndon Johnson got her nickname after the family cook called her "purty as a lady bird."

Was there a Mr. Guinness behind the *Guinness Book of World Records*?
Yes. He was head of the company that published the book when it was created by Sir Hugh Beaver, Norris

McWhirter, and Ross McWhirter in September 1954.
The first *Guinness* was published in August 1955.

Who was Miranda, source of the famous Miranda decision?

In 1963, unemployed twenty-two-year-old Ernesto Miranda was arrested for stealing $8 from a bank employee in Phoenix, Arizona. While in custody, he was picked from a lineup by a young woman who said he had kidnapped and raped her. After two hours of interrogation, the police gained a confession from Miranda. The U.S. Supreme Court threw out the confession because Miranda had not been advised of his right against self-incrimination.

What is Malcolm X's Muslim name? Is it true he didn't write his autobiography?

Born Malcolm Little, the black activist (1925–1965) took the name El-Hajj Malik El Shabazz when he joined the Black Muslims. He broke with the Black Muslims in 1964 and formed a rival group, the Organization of Afro-American Unity. *The Autobiography of Malcolm X*, first published in the year of his death, was ghostwritten by Alex Haley.

Who were the Chicago Seven?

The men who were found innocent of inciting riots during the 1968 Democratic National Convention were: Rennie Davis, David Dellinger, John Froines, Tom Hayden, Abbie Hoffman, Jerry Rubin, and Lee Weiner.

How long was J. Edgar Hoover in charge of the FBI?

Hoover directed the Bureau of Investigation (renamed the Federal Bureau of Investigation in 1935) for 48 years—from 1924 until his death in 1972.

Who said, "Whenever I feel like exercise, I lie down until the feeling passes"?

Although there are many likely candidates, the source is Robert Maynard Hutchins (1899–1977), former president and chancellor of the University of Chicago, dean of the Yale Law School, and chairman of the board for the *Encyclopaedia Britannica*.

Who said, "A little knowledge is a dangerous thing"?

The line is from English writer Alexander Pope's poem *An Essay on Criticism*, and it actually reads "A little learning is a dangerous thing."

Who coined the slogan America—Love It or Leave It?

The slogan was invented by columnist Walter Winchell (1897–1972) in 1940.

Who first said, "You can never be too rich or too thin"?

The rich and thin Duchess of Windsor, the former Wallis Warfield Simpson (1896–1986).

Who said, "We are all worms, but I do believe that I am a glowworm"?

Sir Winston Churchill (1874–1965). The remark fits.

Who was known as the Mouth That Roared?

Martha Mitchell, wife of Richard M. Nixon's attorney general, John Mitchell. She was so called for her sometimes outrageous comments on liberals, protestors, reporters, and other menaces to society.

Was John Bardeen the only person to win two Nobel Prizes in his or her field?

Yes. John Bardeen (b. 1908) won two Nobel Prizes in physics. In 1956, he and W.B.S. Shockley and W. H. Brattain were awarded the prize for the invention of the transistor. In 1972, he and L. N. Cooper and J. R. Schrieffer were awarded the prize for developing the BCS theory, which uses physics to explain superconductivity.

Who is on record as the longest-lived person in the world?

Shigechiyo Izumi of Japan was 120 years old when he died on February 21, 1986. He was born on June 29, 1865. Unproven claims have been made for other people, but Izumi is the oldest for whom there is verification.

· 25 ·

WORLD CULTURES

◆◆◆◆◆

Why do men button from the right, women from the left?
Custom. Men usually dressed themselves, and because most men are right-handed, buttoning from the right made sense. Women were more often dressed by maids, and maids found it easier to work from their right, the wearer's left.

Why do boys wear blue? Why do girls wear pink?
From ancient times, the color blue was considered a precaution against evil spirits—since blue was the color of the heavenly sky. Dressing a baby boy in blue protected him from the evil spirits who wanted to cause him harm. Since girls were considered inferior, it was assumed that evil spirits would not bother with them, and they were dressed in any old color. Much later, people became conscious of the lack of a special color for girls, and pink became standard.

Where did bananas originate?

Not in South America. Bananas first grew in tropical Asia and were eaten by the ancient Greeks and Romans. Banana plants were transported from the Canary Islands off northwest Africa to the Americas soon after the New World was discovered.

Did Eskimos ever live in igloos?

Yes. Canadian Eskimos used igloos as temporary winter homes or camp dwellings. Igloos were usually made of blocks of hard-packed snow, but sometimes of sod, stone, or wood. Most Eskimos now live in more modern dwellings, but igloos can still be found in the area between the Mackenzie River delta and Labrador.

When did people first drink tea?

The beverage originated in China around 2700 B.C. It became popular in England, Holland, and America by the early eighteenth century A.D.

> *When did the British custom of afternoon tea originate?*
> It was introduced about 1840 by the Duchess of Bedford.

> *When was iced tea introduced?*
> It was first offered at the 1904 world's fair, called the Louisiana Purchase Exposition, by Richard Blechynden.

Who were the first coffee drinkers?

Arabian philosopher and physician Avicenna introduced coffee as a beverage about A.D. 1000. He called the drink *bunc*; he believed it to be useful as a medicinal tonic. Not until about the sixteenth century did coffee become accepted as a social beverage in Arabia and Persia.

Why are elbows supposed to stay off the table?

In days of old, tables were generally more crowded during mealtime and one's elbows could get in the way of other diners. Today elbows are allowed on the table by certain etiquette authorities, but the general idea of keeping elbows away from dinnerware and other diners is still a good one.

What are the known forms of marriage?

There are four: monogamy, polygyny, polyandry, and group marriage. *Monogamy* is one wife, one husband. *Polygyny* is one husband, several wives. *Polyandry* is one wife, several husbands. *Group marriage* is several wives, several husbands. Group marriage is by far the rarest and has never been the prevailing form of marriage in any known society.

What is the Napoleonic Code? Is it still binding in New Orleans?

The Code Napoléon is the French civil code enacted in 1804 and introduced into areas then under French control. New Orleans, by that time, was under U.S. control, but the Louisiana state civil code of 1825 (still in effect, with modifications) was influenced by the French code. The Napoleonic Code covered everything from civil rights to the property rights of spouses—the area of greatest interest to Stanley Kowalski in the Tennessee Williams play *A Streetcar Named Desire*, set in New Orleans.

What country has the highest number of physicians? Psychiatrists and psychologists? Dentists?

There are more physicians in the USSR than anywhere else. The United States holds top honors for psychiatrists, psychologists, and dentists.

What is the world's largest office building?

The largest—though not the tallest—is the World Trade Center in New York City. Each of its twin towers contains 4.37 million square feet of space.

What is the most widely cultivated plant?

Wheat, the food base of Western civilization, is by far the most widely grown plant. It has been cultivated for more than 7,000 years in every continent except Antarctica.

What country first introduced income tax?

For 41 years, under the reign of the Medicis, citizens of Florence, Italy, paid what we now know as an income tax. Called the *Scala*, the tax was instituted in 1451, supposedly on a progressive scale. The tax turned into an easy type of political blackmail, and as such it was repealed when the court of the Medicis was overthrown in 1492.

Why do soldiers wear khaki?

Because of Lieutenant Harry Burnett of the Queen's Own Corps of Guides. In December 1846, the English officer was told to develop a "mud-colored" uniform that would camouflage soldiers in dusty surroundings. By early 1847, Burnett had clothed his troops in the light-colored uniform named *khaki*, which comes from the Persian *khak*, meaning "dust" or "ashes." On May 25, 1857, the British 52nd Regiment became the first regular division to sport khakis.

When did the military practice of camouflage come into more general use?

It became standard practice in World War I, when airplanes were used to reconnoiter enemy encampments and to direct artillery fire. Armies found it necessary to camouflage uniforms, helmets, and equipment with the colors of leaves and brush.

What nations belong to NATO? Which of them are part of the Common Market?

The original members of the North Atlantic Treaty Organization, formed in 1949 during the Soviet blockade of Berlin, were: Belgium, Canada, Denmark, France, Iceland, Italy, Luxembourg, the Netherlands, Norway, Portugal, the United Kingdom, and the United States. Greece and Turkey joined NATO in 1952; the Federal Republic of Germany in 1953; and Spain in 1982. The European Economic Community, or Common Market, was founded in 1958. Its original members were: Belgium, France, the Federal Republic of Germany, Italy, Luxembourg, and the Netherlands. Denmark, Ireland, and the United Kingdom joined in 1973; Greece in 1981; and Spain and Portugal in 1986.

What countries are members of OPEC?

In 1960, the Organization of Petroleum Exporting Countries was founded to unify the members' petroleum policies and regulate prices. The founding members were: Iran, Iraq, Kuwait, Saudi Arabia, and Venezuela. Since then, the following nations have also become members: Algeria, Ecuador, Gabon, Indonesia, Libya, Nigeria, Qatar, and the United Arab Emirates.

Who supplies the world with uranium, the main ingredient in atomic weaponry?

As of the early 1980s, the United States held the largest supply, with nearly 27 percent of the world's uranium reserves. Other countries with large supplies were: Australia, with 18 percent; Sweden, with 16 percent; South Africa, with 15 percent; and Canada, with 9 percent.

What are the four humors?

The medieval term refers to what were thought to be the primary bodily fluids: blood, phlegm, yellow bile, and black bile. These represented a human's four basic temperaments: sanguine, phlegmatic, choleric, and melancholic. The idea remained popular into the Elizabethan Age.

What did Adam Smith mean by the "invisible hand" of economics?

According to Adam Smith (1723–1790), it is competition that regulates the marketplace. He first made this observation in *An Inquiry into the Nature and Causes of the Wealth of Nations* (1776).

What are the liberal arts?

The term—which arose in the Middle Ages from the Latin *artes liberales*—refers to the seven branches of learning: logic, rhetoric, arithmetic, geometry, music, astronomy, and grammar. The number seven derives from a quote in Proverbs 9:1: "Wisdom hath builded her house, she hath hewn out her seven pillars."

Where do we get angora wool?

Not from sheep. Angora is harvested from a domesticated rabbit of the same name. The wool is white, black, blue, or fawn. The rabbits are sheared every three months; each one yields about 12 ounces of wool annually. The rabbits first appeared in the eighteenth century in France.

When did pajamas become popular in the Western world?

British colonials from India brought them to their home country about 1870, at which time they became

274 • *The Book of Answers*

popular. Women began wearing pajamas in the early years of the twentieth century, initially as garments for sleeping and later as loungewear.

Are geishas prostitutes?

Not necessarily. A geisha is a member of a professional class of Japanese women who provide entertaining company for men—particularly businessmen. Some geishas sing, dance, or play instruments; most are skilled only at conversation.

Where does Gouda cheese come from?

The original cheese comes from the city of Gouda in the western Netherlands, chartered in 1272.

What is the oldest lighthouse still in use?

The Tower of Hercules, outside La Coruña, Spain. The 185-foot-tall working lighthouse dates from the reign of the Roman emperor Trajan, A.D. 98–117.

What language do Belgians speak? Where is the country located?

The official languages of Belgium are Flemish Dutch and French. The country is bounded by the North Sea, the Netherlands, West Germany, Luxembourg, and France.

How many people speak Basque?

About 700,000 people speak Basque. Most of them live in a narrow area of about 3,900 square miles in Spain and France. Basque is not Indo-European; it is the only remnant of the languages spoken in south-western Europe before the region was Romanized.

Where did the Gypsies originate?

Probably India. Romany, the Gypsy language, is Indic; but it is not known when or why the Gypsies left India. Living as aliens in every country, they reached Persia by A.D. 1000 and northwest Europe by the fifteenth and sixteenth centuries.

What do Gypsies call themselves?

Rom, or "man." Not knowing the origin of Rom, the English called them Gypsies (derived from *Egyptians*); the French, Bohemians; the Spanish, Flemish; and the Swedes, Tatars.

What does *kosher pareve* mean?

It means food that is neutral—that is, fruits, vegetables, and eggs—and can be eaten with either meat or dairy products. The two other main categories of kosher food are *milchig* (dairy) and *fleishig* (meat).

What was the rum ration?

It was an allotment of the liquor apportioned daily to members of the British navy. The practice, introduced in 1731, was discontinued on August 1, 1970.

Who can be buried in Westminster Abbey?

There are no fixed rules that only royalty or noted public leaders may be interred there. The decision rests solely in the hands of the deans of the Abbey.

How old is the Associated Press?

The news agency was organized in 1848.

Where does the United States rank in population?

In 1989, the United States was the fourth most populous country. The top five ran as follows:

1. *China.* 1.104 billion
2. *India.* 835 million
3. *USSR.* 289 million
4. *United States.* 248.8 million
5. *Indonesia.* 184.6 million

Which continent is the most populous?

Asia, by far. Its population in 1989—including the Soviet Union's—was estimated at 3.35 billion. The next most populous continent, Africa, had only 646 million people. Antarctica, the least populous continent, is virtually uninhabited.

· 26 ·

WORLD HISTORY

✦✦✦✦✦

When did the Trojan War occur?

According to scholars, it took place during the thirteenth century B.C. *The Iliad*, Homer's epic account of
the war, is thought to have been written in the ninth
century B.C.

What was the Code of Hammurabi?

The oldest legal code, developed circa 1950 B.C. during
the reign of Babylonian leader Hammurabi, is now
known for its emphasis on the law of retaliation (an eye
for an eye).

When were the 10 lost tribes of Israel lost?

The kingdom of Israel, formed in 930 B.C. by 10 of the
original 12 Hebrew tribes, was conquered by the Assyrians in 721 B.C. Those 10 tribes were exiled and
assimilated into other nations, and so vanished from

history. The other two tribes, founders of the separate
kingdom of Judah, lived on.

When was the Babylonian Exile?

It took place in the sixth century B.C., after the Babylonians conquered the kingdom of Judah. Not all Jews
were deported to Babylonia; in fact, there were several
deportations, each one occurring after an uprising. The
date of the first deportation was probably 597 or 586
B.C. The exile ended in 538 B.C., when the Persian
emperor Cyrus the Great, conqueror of Babylon, allowed the Jews to return home.

In what year was the Temple in Jerusalem destroyed?

It was destroyed twice. The first Temple was razed by
the Babylonians in 586 B.C. The second was destroyed
by the Romans in A.D. 70.

At the time of the Persian Wars, in the sixth century B.C., how large was the Persian Empire?

It was about as large as the continental United States.
Under its Achaemenid rulers, the Persian Empire encompassed not only Persia but Asia Minor, Meso-
potamia, Egypt, and much of modern Afghanistan.
The wars between Greece and Persia lasted from 499 to
479 B.C., ending in Greek victory.

After World War I, how large was the British Empire?

After World War I, the British Empire, or Common-
wealth, covered over 14 million square miles and domi-

nated 450 million people. It encompassed a quarter of the world's population and land surface. Among the countries under its dominion were: Antiqua, Australia, Canada, Ceylon, India, Iraq, Ireland, and Pakistan.

How populous was ancient Athens?

About 300,000 persons lived in the city during the Age of Pericles—slightly less populous than modern Albuquerque, New Mexico, with its 330,000-plus inhabitants.

When was the Ch'in dynasty?

This first great Chinese empire ran from about 221 to 206 B.C. It established the approximate boundaries and governmental system of China for the next 2,000 years, and gave its name to the nation. The effects of the dynasty lasted until the 1911 revolution, which overthrew the empire and created a republic.

Where did the Silk Road run?

The 4,000-mile trade route joined the ancient kingdoms of China and Rome. It started in Sian, followed the Great Wall of China to the northwest, bypassed the Takla Makan Desert, crossed the Pamir Mountains, passed through Afghanistan, and ended at the Levant. Goods were then transported across the Mediterranean Sea to Greece and Rome. The Silk Road is now partially preserved as a highway.

What was the year that put the Ides of March on the calendar?

It was in 44 B.C. that Julius Caesar was assassinated. The date was March 15—the Ides of March.

Who in Rome actually wore togas?

Roman citizens wore the woolen garment when they were in public. There were three types of togas: the *toga picta*, embroidered with golden stars and worn by emperors and victorious generals; the *toga virilis*, the unadorned white toga worn by males fifteen and older; and the *toga praetexta*, bordered in purple and worn by children, magistrates, citizens practicing sacred rites, and others.

How many cities were destroyed by the eruption of Mount Vesuvius?

Three—Pompeii, Herculaneum, and Stabiae, all southeast of modern Naples.

> *When were the ruins of Pompeii discovered?*
> Destroyed in A.D. 79, the city was not discovered until the late 1500s. Formal excavation did not begin until 1748.

What does the name Attila—as in Attila the Hun—mean?

The name for the man described by sixth-century historian Jordanes as "short of stature, with a broad chest and a large head" means "Little Father." Attila was born circa 406 and died in 453.

How long did the Holy Roman Empire last?

An attempt to revive the Roman Empire of the West, the Holy Roman Empire was founded by Charlemagne in A.D. 800. Surviving for more than a thousand years, this entity was not formally abolished until 1806, when it dissolved under pressure from Napoleon.

What was the Truce of God?

It was an attempt by the Roman Catholic Church in 1041 to limit war. In this decree, the Church proposed that no country do battle between Lent and Advent, as well as from the Thursday to the next Monday of important festivals. Although the Lateran Council approved the truce in 1179 and several European countries agreed to it, it did not have much effect.

How many Children's Crusades were there?

Two, both in A.D. 1212. In the first, a French peasant boy named Stephen of Vendôme led thousands of children toward Palestine to free the Holy Land; they were either shipwrecked or sold into slavery. In the same year, a boy preacher named Nicholas led thousands of German children as far as Italy; they were turned back, and many died of hunger and disease.

How long was the Hundred Years' War?

This conflict between France and England for control of France took place over a period of 116 years—from 1337 to 1453—with peaceful intervals of varying length. The French won.

How long did the Spanish Inquisition last?

About 350 years. It was begun in 1478 by Queen Isabella of Castile to search out converted Jews secretly practicing their original faith. In 1483, it was broadened as a means of persecuting any and all heretics. The Spanish Inquisition was not completely abolished until 1834.

Why is America not named after Columbus?

Columbus did not realize he had discovered a new continent, but Amerigo Vespucci, who explored the New World between 1497 and 1504, did. German mapmaker Martin Waldseemüller first applied the name to the new continent on a map published in 1507.

Who was the first man to circumnavigate the earth in one voyage?

Sir Francis Drake (1545–1596) in 1580. His predecessor, Ferdinand Magellan (c. 1480–1521), started such a trip but died before the last of his ships finished the voyage.

How long was the Elizabethan Age?

It ran for the 45 years of the reign of Elizabeth I of England, from 1558 to 1603.

How did the names Whig and Tory arise?

The names of these two English political parties were each invented by the respective party's rival as a pejorative term. The Country Party, representing the merchants and middle class, called their opponents *tories*, a word for Irish plunderers. The Court Party, representing the aristocrats, squires, and Anglican clergy, called their opponents *whigs*, or Scottish cattle rustlers.

When was the Great Fire of London?

It happened in September 1666. The worst fire in London's history, it destroyed many civic buildings and churches, along with 13,000 houses.

When was the Charge of the Light Brigade?

On October 25, 1854, during the Crimean War, James Thomas Brudenell, Seventh Earl of Cardigan, led the British cavalry against the Russians in the Battle of Balaklava. The charge was disastrous, but it did inspire the admiration of the British public—particularly that of Alfred, Lord Tennyson, who wrote the 1855 poem "The Charge of the Light Brigade" in its honor. And although it is not certain whether the cardigan sweater, named for the fashion-conscious earl, was worn at the charge, Brudenell reportedly developed it during this war.

When did Krakatoa, west of Java, explode?

Krakatoa, located in the Sunda Strait between Java and Sumatra, erupted on August 27, 1883. Four hours later, the sound of the eruption could be heard nearly 3,000 miles away; 10 days later, volcanic dust fell at points more than 3,000 miles away.

What was the first nation to grant women the vote?

The self-governing colony of New Zealand gave women the right to vote on September 19, 1893.

Ninety thousand women voted in their first election on November 28, 1893.

> *What was the last Western country to grant women the vote?*
> Switzerland, in 1971.

When was Bloody Sunday?

The Russian Bloody Sunday was January 9, 1905, when a workers' march on the czar's Winter Palace was cut down by cossacks. About a thousand people were killed or wounded; the event sparked the Revolution of 1905. The Irish Bloody Sunday took place on January 30, 1972, when British soldiers shot and killed 13 Catholics in Londonderry, Northern Ireland, during a parade.

Where did the name Bolshevik come from?

In Russian, it means "those of the majority," and it was used by a wing of the Russian Social-Democratic Workers' Party led by V. I. Lenin after they had gained a temporary majority on the party's central committee in 1903. The Bolsheviks believed in a disciplined, centralized party of professional revolutionaries. They called their opponents in the party Mensheviks—"those of the minority."

What were the birth names of Lenin, Trotsky, and Stalin?

Vladimir Ilyich Lenin (1870–1924) was born V. I. Ulyanov. Leon Trotsky (1879–1940) was born Lev

Davidovich Bronstein. Josef Stalin (1879–1953) was born Josef Dzhugashvili.

How many people died on the *Titanic?*

There were between 1,490 and 1,635 deaths in the April 19, 1912, disaster, 100 of whom were women.

How much damage was done on Kristallnacht?

The Nazi anti-Jewish demonstrations of November 9 and 10, 1938, destroyed 815 shops and 29 warehouses. Fires were set to 171 dwellings and 191 synagogues, with 76 other buildings completely destroyed by fire.

In the Nazi army, what was the difference between the Brownshirts and the Blackshirts?

The Brownshirts were the ordinary soldiers; the Blackshirts were members of the army chosen to be bodyguards for high-ranking officials and supervisors of concentration camps. The latter were also known as the SS, short for *Schutzstaffel*, or elite guard.

Were Adolf Hitler and Eva Braun ever married?

He married her on the eve of their joint suicide, which took place on April 30, 1945. They had met in the early 1930s, when she was a saleswoman in the Munich shop of Hitler's photographer, Heinrich Hoffman. Braun became Hitler's lifelong mistress, though she was never allowed to appear in public with him.

What does the *D* in D Day stand for?

D Day is a standard military term referring to the day set for the beginning of an attack. The *D* stands for "Day" (Day-Day). Similarly, the time for an attack is H-Hour (Hour-Hour). The most famous D Day—the Allied invasion of Normandy—took place on June 6, 1944.

What was the "bulge" in the Battle of the Bulge?

It was a break in the Allied lines caused by a German advance in the Ardennes forest in Luxembourg and Belgium, beginning on December 16, 1944. The Germans advanced 50 miles on a 50-mile-long front. On December 26, the Allies began to push the Germans back, and by the end of January 1945, the bulge in the lines had disappeared.

At what time of day did V-E Day occur? V-J Day?

Germany surrendered unconditionally to the Western allies and Russia at 2:41 A.M., French time, on Monday, May 7, 1945. In the United States, this was 8:41 P.M., Eastern Wartime, on Sunday, May 6, 1945. Japan unconditionally surrendered through a note delivered to the U.S. State Department at 6:10 P.M. on Tuesday, August 14, 1945.

Who was sentenced to death at the Nuremberg war crimes trial?

On October 1, 1946, in Nuremberg, 12 of the original 24 defendants were condemned to death by hanging.

They were: Hermann Göring, Joachim Ribbentrop, Field Marshal General Wilhelm Keitel, Ernest Kaltenbrunner, Dr. Albert Rosenberg, Hans Frank, Wilhelm Frick, Julius Streicher, Fritz Sauckel, Colonel General Alfred Jodl, and Arthur Seyss-Inquart. Martin Bormann, who succeeded Rudolf Hess as deputy führer, was tried in absentia and also sentenced to death.

How many sites did the United Nations occupy before moving to its present location?

Four—three of them in New York. The first regular session of the General Assembly was held in October 1945 at Central Hall in London. The United Nations then moved to Hunter College in the Bronx, before establishing interim headquarters at Lake Success on Long Island in August 1946. The New York City building from the 1939 World's Fair in Flushing Meadow, Queens, was subsequently used by the General Assembly. Not until 1951 did the Secretariat Building at Forty-seventh Street and First Avenue, New York City, become the UN's permanent address.

How many people have been secretary-general of the United Nations?

Five. With their countries of origin and terms of office, they are:

Trygve Lie, Norway (1946–1952)
Dag Hammarskjöld, Sweden (1953–1961)

U Thant, Burma (1961–1971)
Kurt Waldheim, Austria (1972–1981)
Javier Pérez de Cuéllar, Peru (1982–present)

What countries today have nuclear weapons?

Eight countries are currently known or suspected to have nuclear weapons. They are: China, France, India, Israel, South Africa, the Soviet Union, the United Kingdom, and the United States.

What was the second country to develop atomic weapons and when did it do so?

On Friday, September 23, 1949, President Truman announced: "We have evidence that within recent weeks an atomic explosion occurred in the USSR."

For whom was the Marshall Plan named? How much money did it extend to Europe?

Named for U.S. Secretary of State George C. Marshall and formally known as the European Recovery Program, the Marshall Plan expended $12.5 billion in U.S. loans and grants to help rebuild Europe after World War II. Payments were made in the fiscal years 1949 through 1952.

How old is the PLO?

The Palestine Liberation Organization—which now claims to represent 4 million Palestinians—was founded in 1964 to unify splintered Palestinian organizations.

Whom did Muammar al-Qaddafi depose to come to power in Libya?

As a colonel in the Libyan army, Qaddafi deposed King Idrīs I in a military coup in September 1969. In the following years, he expropriated Libya's Jewish and Italian communities and nationalized foreign-owned petroleum assets.

When was Bangladesh founded?

In 1971. Formerly East Bengal and then East Pakistan, it rebelled against Pakistan—with help from India—in 1971 but was not recognized by Pakistan until 1974.

How long was the Berlin Wall?

The wall that ran through Berlin was 26.5 miles long. It was put up on the night of August 12–13, 1961. Its function as a barrier between East and West Germany ended on November 9, 1989, when the East German government declared an end to restrictions on emigration and travel to the West.

• 27 •

Twelve Trick
Questions and
Popular Delusions

♦♦♦♦♦

Are poinsettias poisonous?
Despite rumors that the slightest nibble on this
Christmas flower will result in death, poinsettias are
not poisonous to humans. The U.S. Consumer Product Safety Commission determined in 1975 that the
toxicity of poinsettias is a myth, though the flower is a
nonfood substance and, if eaten, could cause some
discomfort.

Where are Panama hats made?
Always and still in Ecuador, where their manufacture
helps to support the economy. They were once distrib-
uted through Panama.

Were red M&M's ever made with a carcinogenic dye?

No. In 1976, M&M/Mars responded to publicity about the carcinogenic effects of red dye number 2 by taking red M&M's off the market. However, red M&M's were not made with red dye number 2: The company acted because people wrongly believed that the dye was being used. Red M&M's have since been reintroduced.

What kind of snake tempted Eve?

It could have been any kind—or none at all. Eve was tempted by a "serpent"—which, in Biblical times, could refer to any creeping animal, particularly if it was venomous. Thus, Eve could have been tempted by anything from a snake to a salamander to a crocodile.

Where in the Bible does it say that cleanliness is next to godliness?

Nowhere. It came from John Wesley (1703–1791), the British theologian who founded Methodism.

Who said, "Everybody talks about the weather, but nobody does anything about it"?

It was not Mark Twain. The quote first appeared in an editorial in the *Hartford Courant* of August 24, 1897, probably written by associate editor Charles Dudley Warner. Warner had collaborated with Twain on *The Gilded Age* (1873).

What were Nathan Hale's last words?

Legend claims that when sentenced to death in 1776 by the British for spying, he proclaimed, "I only regret that I have but one life to lose for my country." But British officer Captain Frederick Mackenzie reports in his diaries that Hale said, "It is the duty of every good officer to obey any orders given him by his commander in chief."

In what Shakespeare play does a character say, "Alas poor Yorick, I knew him well"?

In none of them. In *Hamlet*, Act V, Scene 3, Hamlet says, "Alas, poor Yorick! I knew him, Horatio." For some reason the incorrect version is the one most people remember.

Does Bismarck, North Dakota, have anything to do with Otto von Bismarck, first chancellor of the German Empire?

Yes. The city in south central North Dakota—now the state capital—was founded in 1872 as Camp Hancock. A military post, it protected the crews working on the Northern Pacific Railway. In 1873, it was renamed in honor of then-chancellor Otto von Bismarck in hopes of attracting German railroad investors.

Why is the famous clock called Big Ben?

Big Ben is not a clock. It is a 13.5-ton bell in the clock tower of England's Houses of Parliament. Cast in 1858, the bell's installation was directed by the rotund

Sir Benjamin Hall, commissioner of works. The bell was originally to be called Saint Stephen's, but the British newspapers renamed it Big Ben.

What part of a cat does catgut come from?

This basic element of tennis rackets and violins comes not from cats but from the intestines of sheep. The *cat* in the word may have derived from *kit*, an old word for a small violin. Valued for its toughness, catgut is also used for artificial limbs and in small machines like type-writers and clocks.

Did Neil Armstrong say, "That's one small step for man, one giant leap for mankind"?

That's what it sounds like on the tape that was recorded at 10:56 P.M. (EST) on July 20, 1969. But what he intended to say was, "That's one small step for *a* man, one giant leap for mankind." The *a* was somehow lost in the transmission.

Index

♦ ♦ ♦

Aaron, Hank, 715th home run, 228–229

Abacus, invention of, 103–104

Academy Awards. *See* Oscar(s)

Accidents, household, 113

Acre, area of, 59

Actors. *See* Movie star(s)

Adam and Eve Day, on medieval church calendar, 91

Adam's apple, 99

Adonis, Tammuz and, 144

Adulthood, legal, 117

Advertisement, first personal, 70

Aeschylus, plays of, 121

Ain't, use of word, 60

Air conditioner, invention, 108

Air dance, 38

Airline, first passenger, 75

Airplane(s)
    black box, 116
    first used by U.S. armed forces, 75

Alaska
    Juneau, as largest city in area, 18
    Mount McKinley, elevation, 22
    Point Barrow, as northernmost point, 21

"Alas poor Yorick, I knew him well," 292

Album, first gold, 161

Alexander the Great, empire span of, 195

Algonquin Round Table, persons who sat at, 130–131

Alka-Seltzer, invention, 239

Alligator, crocodile vs., 28

Alphabet, letters least frequently used, 47–48
    most frequently used, 47
    oldest, 47
    vowels, words that use all five, 62

Ambergris, 34

America—Love It or Leave It (slogan), 265

America, naming of, 282

American Revolution
    American casualties, 4
    Americans who fought for British, 4
    regimental composition, 4

American Tragedy, An, actual case behind, 130

Andersonville Prison, deaths at, 9

Andrews, Julie, 167

Angora wool, 273

Animal(s)
    bringing bad fortune, 134
    color vision, 26
    endangered species, first in U.S., 32
    largest living, 30

Annuit Coeptis, on $1 bill, 117

Antarctica, ice thickness, 81

Anthropophagy, 57

Antilles, islands of, 82

Apocalypse, Four Horsemen of, 187

Apollo (Greek god), parents, 135

Apple of one's eye, 99

Arbor Day, first observance, 93
Arbuckle, Fatty, 156
Archer fish, 34
Arctic Circle, determining location, 84
Ark of the Covenant, 191
Armed forces
    first female general in, 73
    presidents who served in, 252
Armstrong, Neil, 293
Arnaz, Desi, 163
Arnold, Benedict, 5
Art Deco, origin of name, 68
Art, famous auto-destructive work, 69
Asia, derivation of name, 79
Asimov, Isaac
    first book, 133
    number of books written by, 133
"Ask not what your country can do for you; ask what you can do for your country," 250
Aspirin, origin, 106
Assembly-line production, introduction, 107
Associated Press, age of, 276
"As Time Goes By" (song), 161
Astronauts
    first on moon, 178
    original seven, in U.S. space program, 178
Athens, Greece
    ancient, population, 279
    first modern Olympics held in, 221
Atomic weapons, development, 288
Attic, origin, 52
Attila, 280
Audits, IRS, in average year, 19
Auld lang syne, 91
Aunt Jemima, reality, 234
Avatar, Hindu meaning, 187
Avenue of the Americas, 151
Avon Lady, and Stratford-upon-Avon, 234

Babies, delivery by stork, 136
Babylonian Exile, 278
Baby Ruth (candy), naming, 239
Bacchanalia, last legal, 145
Bacon, bringing home the (phrase), 50
Baker's dozen, origin, 51
Balding, causes, 98
Balkan Peninsula, countries, 86

Ball, Lucille, 163
Baltimore chop (baseball term), 220
Balto the Wonder Dog, 262
Bananas, origin, 268
Band-Aid, invention, 237–238
Band, to beat the (phrase), origin, 62
Bangladesh, founding, 289
Bank robbery, largest on record, 39
Bardeen, John, 266
Barker, Ma, 45
Baron (British), rank of, 197
Baroque, rococo vs., 65
Barrister, solicitor vs., 58
Bartlett's Familiar Quotations, women quoted in, 117
Baseball
    All-Star game, first, 224
    first recorded game, 219
    longest game on record, 228
    night game, first, 224
    pitching mound, 221
    seventh-inning stretch, 219
    stealing home, record for, 225
    ways to reach first base, 230
    weight of official ball, 230
Baseball Hall of Fame, induction into, 224
Basketball
    first pro player over seven feet, 226
    highest scoring pro game, 227
Basketball hoop, height, 230
Basque (language), 274
Bathos, pathos vs., 122
Batman, 159
    film versions, 167–168
Battle of the Bulge, 286
Bears, formal name for groups, 27
Beatles
    earlier names for, 166
    number of singles in 1964, 166
Beatrice (character), in *Divine Comedy*, 122
Beaver
    number needed for fur coat, 113
    trees cut down by, 29
Beaver State, state known as, 84
Bedlam, and Bethlehem, relationship, 56
Bed, to make a (phrase), origin, 56
Belgium, location and language, 274
Bellevue (hospital), 2
Ben-Gurion, David, nationality, 201
Berkowitz, David Richard, 37
Berlin Wall, length, 289

"Best boy," defined, 171
Best man (phrase), origin, 51
Bethlehem
  bedlam and, relationship, 56
  Star of, 188
Bic pen, origin of name, 241
Big Ben, origin of name, 293
Big Ten, teams constituting, 225–226
Bildungsroman, roman à clef vs., 129
Biltmore clock, New York City, meeting under, 152
Bimonthly meeting, holding of, 174
Birds
  domesticated, most common species, 33
  flying speed, 28
  singing, 28, 31
Births, most popular month, 18
Bismarck, North Dakota, 292
Bismarck, Otto von, 292
Black act, 38
Black Hand, Mafia vs., 36
Black hole, 215
Black liberation flag, meaning of colors, 118
Blackshirts, brownshirts vs., 285
Blarney Stone, kissing, 139
Blind-test, new drug, 217
Blood bank, first, 77
Blood, colors of, 32
Bloody Sunday, 284
Bluebeard, original, 41–42
Blue Hen State, state known as, 83
Blue note, 69
Boat, ship vs., 58
Body heat, loss of, 102
Bohemia, location, 83
Bolero, 68
Bolshevik, origin, 284
Bond, James
  actors that played, 167
  novels about, author of, 132
  significance of 007 for, 167
Bones
  percentage of in human body, 97
  self-standing, 100
Bonnie and Clyde, John Dillinger vs., 46
Borders, U.S., length, 21
Botticelli. *See* Filipepi, Alessandro di Mariano
Boxing
  bare-knuckle bout, last legal, 220
  first heavyweight championship, 220
Boxing glove, invention, 218
Brahman, Brahmin vs., 186
Brahmin, Brahman vs., 186
Brain, Broca's area, 99
Branding, as punishment for crime, 37
Brannock device, 49
Brass, bronze vs., 210
Brassiere, invention, 107–108
Braun, Eva, 285
Bridge, longest, in world, 85
British Empire, size after World War I, 278–279
British Secret Service, head of, 200
Broca's area, of brain, 99
Bronze, brass vs., 210
Brownshirts, blackshirts vs., 285
Brown v. Board of Education of Topeka, Kansas, 13
Buckingham Palace, builder of, 198
Buck, passing the (phrase), origin, 61
Buddhist Eightfold Path, elements of, 187
Bug Bible, 186
Bugs Bunny, origin of name, 158
Bulls, charging of, 26
Burma, Independence Day in, 94
Burma-Shave signs, creator, 240
Buttoning (clothes), 267
BVD, 238
Byzantine emperor, last, 198
Byzantium, location, 80

Caffeine, lethality, 111
Cain, mark on, 184
Calder, Alexander, first mobile, 68
Calendar, Julian and Gregorian, 209
California, naming, 83
Camel cigarettes, trademark, 236–237
Camouflage, military practice of, 271
Canadian border, length, 21
"Candy is dandy/But liquor is quicker," writer of, 125
Cannibalism, 57
Canonical hours, 189
Canterbury Tales
  number of, 123
  pilgrimage in, 123
Capone, Al (Scarface), 35
  actors who played, 170
Capybara, as largest rodent, 25

Carroll, Lewis, "Alice" books by, 127
Car(s)
  stolen, first, 74
  used-, dealership, first, 74
Cartoon (movie), first showings, 156
Carver, George Washington, study of
  peanut, 213
Casablanca (movie), 161
Casinos, legalization of, in Atlantic
  City, 115
Cassidy, Butch. *See* Parker, Robert
  Leroy
Catch-22, original, 132
Catgut, 293
Catharsis, cathartics vs., 113
Cathartics, catharsis vs., 113
Catherine the Great, death, 198
Catholic Church, saints recognized
  by, 185
Cats
  black, and bad fortune, 134
  formal name for groups, 27
  number of in U.S., 21
  purring, 27
  sex of, determining, 25
Celery City, city known as, 84
Celluloid, invention, 106
Cement City, city known as, 84
Census, U.S., first, 5
Centipede, legs on, 26
Central Park, opening of, to public,
  147
Chain gangs, in America, 39
Chair, invention, 103
Chairman of the Board, entertainer
  known as, 172
Chamberlain, Wilt, 226
Chamois, 107
Chan, Charlie, creator of, 130
Chandler, Raymond, 170
Chanel N°5, naming of, 240
Chaos, original use of word, 136
Charge of the Light Brigade, 283
Charlie Brown (comic strip), father's
  profession in, 165
Chase, Salmon P., 6
Chauvinist, first, 257
Checker, Chubby, origin of name,
  164
Cherubim, seraphim vs., 185
Chewing gum, first, 107
Chicago
  fire of 1871, 9
  founder, 2

Haymarket incident, 11
O'Hare Field, 263
origin of name, 111–112
stockyards in, 10
wind speeds in, 15
Chicago amnesia, 38
Chicago overcoat, 38
Chicago Seven, identity, 264
Chicken, 33
Chihuahua dog, and Mexican state,
  30
China
  December 25 observance in, 95
  last emperor, 199
Chinchilla, number needed for fur
  coat, 113
Ch'in dynasty, 279
Chipmunks, origin of name, 164
"Chopsticks," writer of, 67
Chop suey, 110
Christians, significance of February 2
  for, 92
Christmas
  abbreviating as Xmas, 94–95
  earliest reference to December 25,
    95
  Lord of Misrule and, 91
  trees as part of celebration, 95
Christmas Carol, A, last words of,
  178
Christ. *See* Jesus Christ
Churches, U.S., ordaining of women
  in, 190
Cigarette advertising, television and
  radio ban, 118
Cigarette billboard, Times Square,
  last smoke ring blown from,
  151–152
City(ies), U.S.
  largest in area, 18
  most popular, 18
Cleanliness is next to godliness, 291
Close encounters, of first and second
  kind, 216
Clouds, types of, 204
Cockroach, largest, 26
Coelacanth fish species, age, 25
Coffee drinkers, first, 268
Coffee, first instant, 108
Coins, U.S., In God We Trust motto
  on, 6
Colonies, American, 13
  original, 180
Colors, stereotyping, 267

Color vision, of animals, 26
Common Market, 271–272
Computer, first modern, 109
Conquering Lion. *See* Selassie, Haile
Constipation, long-term, 101
Continental army, regiment
    requirements, 4
Continental Baths, location, 169
Continental Congress, Second, 7
Continental drift, speed, 203
Continental shelf, 204
Continent(s)
    most populous, 276
    number, 80
Cookie, world's best selling, 119
Cosa Nostra, meaning of word, 36
Cosmic year, length, 203
Crab, speed, 26
Cracker Jack, number of peanuts in,
    234
Crap, origin of word, 51
Crime (sports), first pro indicted,
    229
Crocodile, alligator vs., 28
Cronkite, Walter, CBS and, 171
Crows, formal name for groups, 27
Crusades, children's, number of, 281
Cuba
    Independence Day in, 94
    U.S. territories in, 88
Currency, U.S.
    $1 bill, motto on, 117
    dollars and cents in, 6
    female representations on, 7
Cyclops, 136

Dachshund, origin of name, 30
Dada, origin, 67
Dandelion, origin, 53
Da Vinci, Leonardo, *Mona Lisa*
    painting, 64
Day, Doris, 163
D Day, 286
"Dead man's hand," aces and eights
    as, 112
Death rattle, causes, 38
Debates, public, 250–251
Debt, national, increase, 14
December 25, celebrations observed
    on, 95
Declaration of Independence
    opening words, 177
    signers who became president, 246
Deduction, induction vs., 182

Democratic party
    donkey as symbol, 7
    first woman to head, 78
Dempsey, Jack, 223
Denim, in making Levi's jeans, 233
Dentists, country with highest
    number, 270
Department store, first built, 71
Detectives, 43
Detroit, founder, 2
Diamonds
    burning of, 215
    one-carat, weight, 115
Dillinger, John, man who shot, 42
Dinosaur National Monument,
    location, 88
Dinosaurs, extinction, 205
Dionysus (Greek god), parents, 135
Diva, prima donna vs., 69
Divine Comedy (Dante), 122
Divorce rate, marriage rate vs., 19
Dixie Cup, origin of name, 237
Dodgers, Brooklyn
    moving date of, 226
    origin of name, 221–222
Dodo, extinction, 29
Dog days (phrase), 24
Doges of Venice, 197
Dogs
    biting, breeds, 24
    life expectancy, 23
    mating, most unlikely, 34
    number of in U.S., 21
    of presidents, 253
Donkey, as symbol of Democratic
    party, 7
Doppelganger, 129
Double-blind test, new drug, 217
"Dragnet" (TV series), badge
    number of Sgt. Joe Friday, 163
Dr. Pepper, numbers on bottles of,
    241
Dr. Scholl, reality of, 238
Du Sable, Jean Baptiste Pointe, 2

$E=mc^2$, 174
Earl (British), rank, 197
Earth
    circumnavigation of, 282
    formation of, scientists' view, 204
    smallest country on, 82
    surface permanently frozen, 81
    thickness of crust, 205
    unexplored surface of, 81

Earthquake, greatest, 5
Easter Sunday, determining date, 93
Ederle, Gertrude, swimming of English Channel, 223
Edward VIII (king of England), abdication, 199
e.g., i.e. vs., 54
Egypt
  pharaohs, god descended from, 134
  ten plagues, 187–188
86, to (phrase), popularity, 60–61
Einstein, Albert, 214
  law on equivalence of mass and energy, 174
Elbows, on tables, 269
Electric chair, first man to die in, 73
Elephant, as symbol of Republican party, 7
Elevation, highest natural, in New York metropolitan area, 152
Elevations, U.S., highest and lowest, 22
Elevator, first, 105
El Greco. *See* Theotokopoulos, Domenikos
Elizabethan Age, length, 282
Embryo, human, first heartbeat, 100
Empire State Building (New York), 152
  previous structure on site, 150
Employment, in federal agencies, 19
Ensure, use of word, 60
Ermine, number needed for fur coat, 113
Eskimos, use of igloos, 268
et al., et cetera vs., 54
et cetera, et al. vs., 54
E (the letter), book written without use of, 131
"Eureka!," meaning, 207–208
European Recovery Program, 288
Europe, derivation of name, 79
Evert, Chris, tennis stroke, 228
"Everybody talks about the weather, but nobody does anything about it," 291
Eve, snake that tempted, 291
Evolution of man, geologic era of, 204
Eyeglasses, introduction of, in Europe, 105

Fabric brighteners, nonchlorine, 216
Family, female and male side of, 58
Fan, cooling room with, 108
Fathom, depth, 59
FBI (Federal Bureau of Investigation), 265
  length of time in operation, 36
  Ten Most Wanted List, 36
FDIC (Federal Deposit Insurance Corporation), insuring of, 116
Fears, of Americans, 15
Feather, in Yankee Doodle's cap, 3
February 2, significance of for Christians, 92
Feet, measuring device of, for shoes, 49
Fetchit, Stepin, origin of name, 157
Fiat (car), naming of, 235
Fifth column, inventor of term, 59
Figure skating, Olympic medal winner, 224–225
Filipepi, Alessandro di Mariano, 64
"Filthy little atheist," 260
Fingerprints
  acquisition of, on fetus, 100
  function, 100
  of identical twins, 100
Fingers
  crossing of, for good luck, 143
  largest number of on one person, 97
Firefly, light from, 217
Fire(s)
  Chicago, of 1871, 9
  of London (1666), 283
  Saint Elmo's, 205
First strike, first use vs., 118
First use, first strike vs., 118
Fish
  age of, determining, 25
  archer, 34
  coelacanth species, 25
  sardines, 29
  Siamese fighting, 31
  sleep habits, 31
Flag, American, designer, 4
Flashback, earliest use of in Western literature, 121
Fleming, Ian, intelligence work of, 132
Flibbertigibbet, definition, 167
Foods, first frozen, 76
Food stamps, recipients, 19

Football
Army-Navy game, first, 220
first pro player, 221
longest game on record, 227
Forbidden Planet, 164
Ford, Gerald R.
public debates, 250–251
real name, 247
WIN buttons and, 14
Forests, national, in U.S., 22
Foreword, preface vs., 59
Fortnight, length, 114
44-Caliber Killer, 37
Four Hundred, New York society, 149
Fox, number of to produce fur coat, 113
Freemasonry, 191
French Foreign Legion, joining, 120
Frogs, jumping range, 33
Frown, number of muscles to, 102
Frusen Gladje, 243
Fuller Brush man, first, 236
Fu Manchu, Dr., archadversary of, 130

Gaga, 52
Galahad, Sir, parents, 139
Gamete, zygote vs., 101
Garbo, Greta, 160
Gardner, Erle Stanley, 131
Perry Mason novels by, 167
Gargoyles, practical function of, 63
Gas chamber, first person to die in, 74
Gases, noble, 213
Gehenna, 192
Gehrig, Lou, consecutive games of, 225
Geishas, 274
General, U.S., first black, 73
Genghis Khan, 196
Geologic time, earliest era of, 204
George III (king of England)
illness, 198
relationship to Victoria, 198
Gerber baby, 238
Geronimo, real name, 259
Gershwin, George and Ira, collaboration between, 157
Gethsemane, location, 186
Gettysburg Address, people present at, 9
Giants, New York, renaming, 226

Gideon Bibles, first hotel to have, 183
Gilbert, W. S., 178
Gilded Age, 9
Gimlet (drink), 259
Girl in the Red Velvet Swing, identity, 260
Gladiatorial combat
abolishment, 218
first, 218
Glass, components, 212
Gluteus minimus, 101
Gnats, formal name for groups, 27
Goldfish, eating of, 160
Golf
grand slam, 223
hole, depth and width, 230
longest drive in PGA history, 227
Gone with the Wind, copies sold, 131
"Good to the last drop," origin, 236
Goody Two-Shoes, original, 256
Googol (number), 214
Goose bumps, reasons for, 100
Gopher State, state known as, 84
Gouda cheese, 274
Gouging (sport), 219
Graces, identification of, 142
Grand Canyon (Arizona), 16
length, 87
popularity, 82
Grand Marnier (drink), 259
Grant, Ulysses S., 9
Grasses, species, 205–206
"Grateful Dead, The" (folktale), 143
Grauman's Chinese Theatre, footprints at, 76
Gravity, Newton's law, 209–210
Great Britain. *See* United Kingdom
Great Expectations, Pip's real name in, 127
Greece, Independence Day in, 94
Groundhog Day, observance, 92
Groundhogs, accuracy of weather predictions, 92
gry, words ending in, 182
Guano, chemical content, 216
Guinness Book of World Records, 263
Gulliver's Travels (Swift), 124
Gunfight at O.K. Corral, 11
Gypsies, origin, 275

Haagen-Daz, 244
Hail, causes, 206–207

Hair(s)
  growth speed, 98
  on human head, 98
  loss of, 98
Hale, Nathan, last words, 292
Halley's comet, observation of, 208
Hamartia, hubris vs., in Greek
  tragedies, 122
Hammurabi, Code of, 277
Handguns, inexpensive, 44
Hanukkah, 96
Harlem, as black neighborhood, 148
Harris, Julie, Tony Awards, 169–
  170
Harvey Wallbanger (drink), 259
Hasidism, founder, 192
Hatfields and McCoys, domicile, 10
Hathaway Shirt, Man in, 243
Hawaiian Islands, eight main islands,
  84
Haymarket incident, 11
Hays Code, institution of, 157–158
Hazardous waste sites, top five states,
  16
Head, human, hairs on, 98
Hearst, Patty, kidnapping, 40
Heartbeats, in lifetime, 98
Heavyweight champion, first black,
  222
Hell, deepest circle of, in Dante's
  Inferno, 122
Hellfire, Gehenna and, 192
Henry VIII, six wives, 180
Hens, egg sitting, 23
Hercules, labors, 139–140
Herods, King, number, 195–196
Hiawatha, tribe of, 126
Hiccuping, longest recorded attack,
  97
Highways
  first coast-to-coast, 75
  numbering of in U.S., 118–119
Hijack, origin of word, 40
Hinduism, "ends of man" in, 186–
  187
Hitler, Adolf, 285
Hobson's choice, 255
Hockey
  goals, record holder for, 227
  puck, size, 231
Hollywood Ten, identifying, 162
Holy Roman Empire, 280–281
Homographs, 55
Homonyms, 55

Homophones, 55
"Honeymooners, The" (TV series)
  Brooklyn street address, 164
  first broadcast, 163–164
  number of episodes filmed, 163
Hoodlum, origin of word, 52
Hopkinson, Francis, 4
Hospital, oldest in U.S., 2
Hostages, American, in Tehran, Iran,
  14
Houdini, Harry, death of, 261
Hour, division into minutes, 115–
  116
Household task, most despised, 22
Houseplants, response to light, 217
"Howdy Doody" (TV series), 165
Hubris, hamartia vs., in Greek
  tragedies, 122
Hula-Hoop, origin, 104
Human body
  parts "fall asleep," meaning, 99
  worth of, 102
Human flesh, eating of, 57
Humble pie, to eat (phrase), origin,
  56
Humors, four, 272
Hundred Years' War, length, 281
Hurricanes, U.S., lives lost in, 212
Hymn-singing, introduction of, 189

Ides of March, year put on calendar,
  279
Id, origin of term, 213
i.e., e.g. vs., 54
"I Love Lucy" (TV series)
  Little Ricky in, 163
  number of seasons, 163
Immaculate Conception, 185–186
Impeachment, articles of, 250
Incense, introduction, 189
Inch, development of, 104
Income, personal, highest per-capita,
  17
Income tax, introduction of, 270
Independence Day, observance, 94
India, last viceroy, 200–201
Indianapolis 500, first, 222
Induction, deduction vs., 182
Inferno (Dante), 122
Infinitives, splitting, 59–60
In God We Trust (motto), 6
In like Flynn (phrase), derivation, 62
Insects, blood color, 32
Insurance City, city known as, 84

Insure, use of word, 60
Internal Revenue Service, audits by, 19
International date line, 86
Intestines, length, 101
"Invisible hand" of economics, 273
Iran, 80
Irregardless, use of word, 60
"I shall never believe that God plays dice with the universe," 214
Ishtar (goddess), 144
Islam, 184
Israel, lost tribes, 277
It Boy, identity, 262
It Girl, identity, 261
Ivory soap, floating of, 232

Jack the Ripper, murders, 37
Jackson, Michael, and Jackson 5, 168
Jane Eyre (Bronte, Charlotte), 173
Jekyll, Dr., and Mr. Hyde, reality of, 127
Jerusalem, Temple in, destruction, 278
Jesus Christ
    birth, 183
    criminals crucified with, 186
    crucifixion, 254
Jews
    excommunication, 192
    meaning of Tammuz to, 144
Johnson, Lady Bird, 263
Journal of the Plague Year (Defoe), year described in, 124
Journeymen Printers Union, strike, 5

Kangaroos
    formal name for groups, 27
    jumping range, 23
Karamazov, Brothers, number, 127
Kemo Sabe, 172
Kennedy, John F., inaugural speech, 250
Keystone Kops, origin, 156
Khaki, wearing of, 271
King, Martin Luther, Jr., 41
Kirk, Captain James T. ("Star Trek"), middle name, 168
Kismet, origin of word, 57
Kisses, greatest number, in single film, 157
Kissing, public, as crime in U.S., 40
Knockout punch, effects, 101
Kodak, origin of name, 235

Kosher food, symbol Ⓤ on, 117
Kosher pareve, 275
Krakatoa, explosion of, 283
K rations, meaning of *K* in, 242
Kristallnacht, damage on, 285
Kublai Khan, 125, 196

Ladies' Mile, New York, 148
Lady of the Lake, identifying, 139
Lakes, five largest, 81
Land of Steady Habits, state known as, 83
Language, wordiest, 117
Last laugh, explanation, 39
Laundromat, first opened, 77
League, distance, 59
Leap year, first, 208
Lebanon, Independence Day in, 94
Lee, Robert E., commands, in Civil War, 8
Legs Diamond. *See* Noland, John T.
Lenin, Vladimir Ilyich, birth name, 284
Leopold and Loeb, whereabouts of, 45
Liberal arts, 273
Liberty Bell(s), number, 3
Lighthouse, oldest in use, 274
Lightning, air temperature and, 206
Light, speed, 211
Lilliputians, enemies of, in *Gulliver's Travels* (Swift), 124
Lincoln, Abraham
    assassination, 247
    Gettysburg Address, 9
Lindbergh, Charles, Pulitzer Prize, 132
"Little knowledge is a dangerous thing, A," 265
Livingstone, David, 260
Lobotomy, development, 214–215
Lobsters, blood color, 32
Log cabin, first president born in, 246
Log Cabin syrup, 233–234
Lolita, age of, at first meeting with Humbert Humbert, 132
London, Great Fire of, 283
Lone Ranger, 172
Longbaugh, Harry, 46
Longest-lived person in world, 266
Looking a gift horse in the mouth (phrase), 62

L.S./M.F.T. (Lucky Strike Means Fine Tobacco), 242
Lucky charm, rabbit's foot as, 135
Lush, origin of word, 50
Luxembourg, size, 88
Lynching, practice, 38

M&M candy, 241
  color breakdown, 241–242
  red dye number 2 and, 291
McDonald's, beef used each year, 244
McGuffey Eclectic Readers, 257
Madison Square Gardens, number of ever existing, 147–148
Mafia
  Black Hand vs., 36
  five families of New York City, 37
  meaning of word, 36
Mail, handled by U.S. Post Office daily, 20
Malapropism, 124
Malaprop, Mrs. (character in *The Rivals*), 124
Malcolm X, muslim name, 264
Mammals
  blood color, 32
  gestation period, shortest, 27
  longest life span, 27
"Man from U.N.C.L.E., The" (TV series), 168
Manhattan Island
  dimensions, 146
  purchase, 1
Manholes, round, reasons for, 113
Manilow, Barry, 169
"Man who ate Democrats, the," 258
Marlowe, Philip (detective), actors who played, 170
Marriage rate, divorce rate vs., 19
Marriages
  known forms, 269
  person with most, 258
Marshall Plan, 288
"Mary Had a Little Lamb," writer of, 126
Mason-Dixon line, 256
Mason, Perry, creator of, 131
Mata Hari, birth name, 261
May Day, as international holiday, 93
Mayor, first black, 73
Mean, median vs., 55
Meat-eater, 39
Mecca, location, 184

Medal of Honor, U.S., female winner, 258
Median, mean vs., 55
Meetings, bimonthly, 174
Meir, Golda, nationality, 201
Menorahs, displaying of, 96
Meteorite, persons hit by a, 115
Mexican border, length, 21
MGM, lion as trademark, 239
MI5 (Britain's counterintelligence service), 43
MI6 (Britain's Secret Service), 43
Michelin Man, name of, 243
Mickey Finn (drink), 259
Midler, Bette, 169
Military, U.S., persons on active duty, 20
Millipede, legs on, 26
Minks, number of to produce fur coat, 113
Minutes of a meeting, derivation of term, 56
Miranda decision, source, 264
Mishnah, age, 191–192
Misrule, Lord of, holiday associated with, 91
Missouri, earthquake in, 5
Moby Dick (Melville), first sentence, 178
Mona Lisa (painting), 64
Monopoly, first in U.S., 71
Moon
  age, 202
  blue, 119
  orbit around earth, 203
  size, 202
Moran, George ("Bugs"), 35
Moriarty, James (Sherlock Holmes' rival), whereabouts, 127–128
Mosquito Coast, location, 86
Mothe Cadillac, Antoine de la, 2
Mother Goose, existence of, 137–138
Mother's Day, origin, 93–94
Mourning, black as color of, 137
Mouth That Roared, 266
Moviemaking, regulation of, 157–158
Movies
  actor appearing in greatest number, 162
  first reviewer, 155
  most violent film, 171
  road pictures, 161–162

story most often made into, 171
winner of most Oscars, 165
Movie star(s)
first, 155
insuring of body assets, 263
most leading roles, 169
Oscars, first to win three, 169
real names, 159–160
stage names, 170–171
Movie theater
drive-in, first, 75
first in United States, 74–75
Mr. Big. *See* Rothstein, Arnold
Mr. Ed, voice of, 165
Muckraker (journalistic term), origin,
128
Muhammad Ali, title bouts, 229
Muscles
gluteus, 101–102
percentage of in human body, 98
to frown or smile, 102
Muses, identification, 140
Mushroom, world's deadliest, 110
Music
blue note, 69
instruments, earliest, 63
12-tone theory, 67
Muslims
calendar, 191
use of prayer rugs by, 189

Napoleonic Code, 269
Nativity Scene, first representation in
art, 63
NATO (North Atlantic Treaty
Organization), 271–272
Navratilova, Martina
birthplace, 229
defection, 229
Navy, U.S., establishment, 7
Neat's-foot oil, use, 231
Needle Park, location, 151
Nereids, Greek sailors like for,
136
Neutrinos, 216
New Orleans, first movie theater in
U.S., 74
New York City
first electric sign in, 148
first explorer to see, 146
five tallest buildings in, 152–153
Miss Subways of, 151
as most popular city, 18
speed limit in, 153

Triangle Waist Company fire in,
149
New York Stock Exchange, opening,
147
NFL (National Football League),
222
Niagara Falls (New York), 16
Nice, derivation of, 48
Nicklaus, Jack, first major
tournament win, 227
Nigeria, Independence Day in, 94
Nightmare, origin of word, 53
Nike (goddess of victory), 141
Nirvana, location, 193
Nixon, Richard M.
resignation, 250
running mate of, in 1960, 178
Noah's ark
animals on, in Bible, 184
size, 183
Nobel Prize
first American to receive, 130
first English writer to receive, 130
for literature, first recipient, 129
for Peace, money supplier for, 112
in physics, winner of two, 266
Noland, John T., nickname, 46
North Pole, black explorer on
expedition to, 261
Nostradamus, predictions, 256
Nouvelle Vague, 165
Novel(s)
by Bronte sisters, 126–127
first American, 126
"Now is the time for all good men to
come to the aid of the party,"
origin, 111
Noxzema, origin of name, 237
Nuclear attack, "push button" for,
251
Nuclear weapons, countries that
have, 288
Nuremberg war crimes trial, 286–
287
Nutrias, description, 31

Ocean abyss, depth, 119
Office building, largest, 270
O'Hare Field, naming, 263
"Oh what a tangled web we weave
when first we practice to
deceive," writer, 174
O.K. Corral, gunfight at, 11
O.K. (the word), 48

"Old soft shoe" (phrase), 154–155
Olympics, first modern, 221
OPEC (Organization of Petroleum Exporting Countries), 272
"Opera ain't over 'til the fat lady sings, the," 231
Opera(s)
  diva and prima donna in, 69
  Gilbert and Sullivan, 178
Orient, largest Chinese settlement outside, 85
Oscar(s)
  movie winning most, 165
  winner of three, first, 169
  youngest person to win, 158
Oswald, Lee Harvey, shooting, 41
Ouija board, 116
Oz, kingdom of, naming, 128

Pacific Ocean, pressure at bottom, 203
Pac-Man, inventor of, 243
Painters, signing of paintings by, 64, 66
Pajamas, popularity, 273–274
Panama hats, manufacture of, 290
Papal bull, 50
Parameter, perimeter vs., in mathematics, 54
Parker, Robert Leroy, 46
Parole violations, number, 42
Pathos, bathos vs., 122
Peace symbol, invention, 119
Peacocks, formal name for groups, 27
"Peanuts" (comic strip), last name of Linus and Lucy in, 165
Pearl Harbor, warning of attack on, 13
Peeping Tom, original, 255
Peerage (Great Britain), line, 197
Pen names, famous, real names behind, 125–126
"Pennsylvania 6-5000" (song), hotel that inspired, 150
Perimeter, parameter vs., in mathematics, 54
Pershing missile, U.S. Army, travel range, 20
Persian Empire, size at time of Persian Wars, 278
Persia. *See* Iran
Petard, hoist by one's (phrase), 48
Philby, Kim (Soviet spy), 42

Philosophers' stone, 142
Physician, country with highest number, 270
Picturesque, 65–66
Piggy bank, origin, 104–105
Pig(s)
  biggest in history, 26
  formal name for groups, 27
  hogs vs., 32
  intolerance to sun, 31
Pilgrims, food at first Thanksgiving, 1
Pinkerton Detective Agency, 43, 257–258
Pin money, 52
Piranhas, eating speed, 29
Pittsburgh, naming, 2
Pittsburgh of the South, city known as, 84
Pixies, 143
Plagues, ten, of Egypt, 187–188
Planets, discovery, 206
Plant
  most widely grown, 270
  world's largest, 205
Plasma
  to geologist, 217
  to physician, 216
  to physicist, 217
Plastic, first manmade, 106
Plastics, 213–214
Pledge of Allegiance, writer, 12
Pliny the Elder, 255
Pliny the Younger, 255
PLO (Palestine Liberation Organization), 288
Pockets, introduction of, 105
Poinsettias, toxicity, 290
Poker, rank of hands in, 174
Polecats, 32
Pole of Inaccessibility, location, 85
Political parties, first woman to head, 78
Polo game, number of players in, 230
Polymers, 213–214
Pompeii, discovery of ruins, 280
Pontius Pilate, 254
Pony Express, 8
Pope(s)
  first three, 184–185
  longest-reigning, 199
  most popular names for, 185
Porphyria (blood disorder), 198

Postage stamp, U.S., first woman commemorated on, 73
Post Office, U.S., average daily mail, 20
Prayer rugs, religion using, 189
Prayer wheel, religion using, 189
Preface, foreword vs., 59
Pre-Raphaelite Brotherhood (PRB), 66
Presidential mansion, U.S., first, 245
President(s)
 with armed forces service, 252
 bachelor, 247
 birthplace of most, 251
 born after U.S. declared independence, 246
 born west of Mississippi, first, 247
 cabinet, executive departments in, 251–252
 carved on Mount Rushmore, 249
 dogs, names, 253
 federal income tax ratification, 247
 first to receive doctorate, 248
 line of succession to, 245
 number assassinated, 249
 shortest office term, 249
 Speaker of House elected as, first, 246
 state capitals named after, 253
Presley, Elvis, first number one hit, 164
Prester John, empire of, 142–143
Pretzel City, city known as, 84
Priapus (Greek god), 141–142
Prima donna, diva vs., 69
"Princess and the Pea, The," number of mattresses in, 143
Prisoners, U.S. on death row, 46
Private eyes, derivation of name, 43–44
Production, assembly-line technique, 107
Prostitution, first house of, 70
Psychiatrists, country with most, 270
Psychologists, country with most, 270
Public opinion poll, first, 71
Pulitzer Prize
 for fiction, first woman to win, 129
 Lindbergh's winning of, 132
Pygmies, location, 116
Pythagorean theorem, 254

Qaddafi, Muammar al-, 289
Quark, origin, 214
Quasar, 215
Quetzalcoatl (Aztec god), 144
Quicksand, 211

Rabbit's foot, as good luck charm, 135
Radio City Music Hall, first and last regular movie in, 150
Radio station, first broadcast, 76
Ragnarok, in Norse mythology, 144–145
Railroad, first chartered, 8
Rainbow, colors making up, 173
Rake's Progress, The, 65
Rathbone, Basil, film roles as Sherlock Holmes, 161
Ravel, Maurice, 68
Ray, James Earl, 41
Record, first gold, 161
Red-light district, naming of, 39
Republican party
 elephant as symbol, 7
 first woman to head, 78
Restaurant, first, 71
Rivers, five longest, 177
Road pictures, of Hope, Crosby, and Lamour, 161–162
Rock of Gibraltar, location, 87
Rococo, baroque vs., 65
Rodent, world's largest, 25
Roman à clef, bildungsroman vs., 129
Rome
 seven hills, 85
 Vatican City, 82
Roosevelt, Franklin D., polio and, 248
Roosevelt, Theodore, 260
Rosary, invention, 190
Rosenbergs, Julius and Ethel, execution, 41
Ross, Betsy, 4
Rothstein, Arnold, 41
Round Table, knights at, 134
Rubber band, invention, 106
Rubber Capital of World, city known as, 84
Rubberneckers, traffic delays and, 111
"Rubbernecking delays" (phrase), 111
Rubik's Cube, inventor, 243

Rulers, longest reigning, 194–195
Rum ration, 270
Rushmore, Mount
    presidents carved on, 249
    size, 69

Sacco and Vanzetti, pardon of, 44
Safety pin, origin, 103
Saint Peter's Basilica, seating at, 64
Saints, number of, recognized by
    Catholic Church, 185
Saint Valentine's Day Massacre, 35
Salary, origin of word, 57
Saltpeter, purpose, 211
Salt, spilling of, as bad luck, 138
San Francisco earthquake, 6
Sanka, origin of name, 235
Santa Claus
    brother of, name, 96
    reindeers, names, 173–174
"Santa Claus Is Comin' to Town"
    (song), first singer, 158
Sardine, 29
Saturday Night Specials, 44
Scapegoat, original meaning, 188
School segregation, Supreme Court
    decision, 13
Scopes trial, decision, 44
Scot free, to go (phrase), origin, 61
Scrabble word, everyone's favorite,
    57
Secretariat, racing career, 228
Selassie, Haile, 199
Semantics, semiotics vs., 55
Semiotics, semantics vs., 55
Senate, U.S., number of members in,
    174
Senator, U.S., first black, 72
Seraphim, cherubim vs., 185
Seven Dwarfs, identifying, 175
Seven Hills of Rome, 85
7UP, origin of name, 240–241
Seven Wonders of the World
    current existing list, 179–180
Sex, world leaders dying while
    having, 255
Shakers, formal name for, 190
Shakespeare, William
    number of sonnets written by, 124
    play of, character "Exits, pursued
        by a bear," 123
Shangri-La
    name changing of, 249
    reality of, 131

Shark attack, largest recorded, 33
Sheep, in White House, 248
Shell Oil, origin of name, 233
Sherwood Forest, location, 89–90
Ship, boat vs., 58
Shoelace, covering on end of, 49
Shoes, instrument to measure feet
    for, 49
Shogun, origin, 196
Shooting stars, 207
Shoplifting, 45
Shopping center, first built, 77
Shorebirds, 31
Showboat, first and last, 114–115
Shrapnel, invention, 106
Shyster, origin of word, 49
Siamese fighting fish, 31
Silicon Valley, size, 88
Silk Road, 279
Sinbad the Sailor, 122
Sins, seven deadly, 175
Sisyphus, punishment of, 140–141
Sixth Avenue, renaming, 151
Skeleton, of average person, 97
Skiing, fastest speed in, 230
Skin
    square feet of, on human body, 97
    wrinkling of in water, 102
Skunks, purpose of scent, 30
Skyscraper, first, 72
Slaves
    African, 3
    freeing, 3
Smile, number of muscles to, 102
Smith, Adam, 273
Snakes, speed, 33
Sneezing, longest recorded attack, 97
Snow White and the Seven Dwarfs
    (Disney), 175
Sojourner Truth's, real name, 257
Solicitor, barrister vs., 58
Solomon (king), reign of, 194
Song(s), most widely sung in
    English-speaking world, 155
"Son of Sam." *See* Berkowitz, David
    Richard
Sooners, origin, 53
Sound of Music, The, Maria in, 167
South Vietnam, surrender of, 13
Spacecraft, first to land on moon, 78
Spanish Inquisition, time span of,
    281
Speleology, 57
Spelunking, 57

Sperm cells, in human ejaculation, 99
Spiders, black widow, 27
Spock ("Star Trek"), parents, 168
Sports
    first publicized event, 223–224
    worst disaster in, 222
Spy(ies)
    slang terms, 43
    Soviet, 42
Stage names, list, 170–171
Stalactite, stalagmite vs., 206
Stalagmite, stalactite vs., 206
Stalin, Josef, birth name, 285
Stanley, Henry Morton, 260
Star of Bethlehem, 188
Stark naked, origin of term, 54
"Star Spangled Banner, The," 12
Stars, visibility of, 207
"Star Trek" (TV series), 168
Stassen, Harold, as presidential
    candidate, 250
State chemists, 39
State electricians, 39
Steel, galvanization of, 210
Stockyards, in Chicago, 10
Stone masonry, 191
Stork, delivery of babies by, 136
Strike, labor, first in U.S., 5
Sullivan, Arthur, 178
Sun
    earth's speed around, 202
    temperature, 202
Sunburn, 31
Sundance Kid. *See* Longbaugh,
    Harry
Superbowl, first, 227
Superman, 159
Supermarket, first, 112
Supernova, energy generated by, 215
Supreme Court, U.S.
    number of justices, 8
    school segregation decision, 13
Survival of fittest (phrase), 211
Swan song, 61
Swastika, meaning of, before
    Hitler,138
Sweatshops, 58
Swine. *See* Pig(s)
Syzygy, 57

Taj Mahal, builder, 256
Tale of Genji, The, 122
Tale of Two Cities, A, first and last
    lines, 179

Tallest person, on record, 258
Talmud, age of, 191–192
Tamburlaine the Great, 197–198
Tammany Hall (New York), naming,
    146–147
Tammuz, 144
Tango, origin, 66
Tantalize, source of word, 141
Tantalus, punishment, 141
Tapeworms, size, 32
Tarantulas, web spinning, 32
Tasmanian devil, description, 33
Tavern-on-the Green, building, 147
Tax, U.S. government's right to, 11
Tea
    afternoon, 268
    iced, 268
    origination of as drink, 268
Teapot Dome scandal, 248–249
Tehran, Iran, American hostages in,
    14
Television
    cigarette advertising ban, 118
    color, invention, 108–109
    first news-broadcast, 77
    longest-running series, 171
Temperature statistics, 144
Ten Commandments, 175–177
Ten Most Wanted List (FBI), 36
Tennis
    grand slam, 225
    stroke, of Chris Evert, 228
Termites, usefulness, 28
Texas leaguer (baseball term), 219–
    220
Thanksgiving
    first, 1
    as national holiday, 94
"That's one small step for man, one
    giant leap for mankind," 293
Them (pronoun), use of, 60
Theotokopoulos, Domenikos, 64
Those (pronoun), use of, 60
"Those who cannot remember the
    past are condemned to repeat it"
    (in Santayana), 128
Three sheets to the wind (phrase), 48
Throat, 99
T.H.R.U.S.H. (Technological
    Hierarchy for the Removal of
    Undesirables and the
    Subjugation of Humanity), 168
Time measurement, 115–116
Times Square, naming, 149

Time zones, in North America, 86
Tin Pan Alley, location, 67
Tipperary, location, 90
" 'Tis better to have loved and lost/
    Than never to have loved at all,"
    125
Titanic, number of deaths, 285
Toes, largest number of on one
    person, 97
Togas, wearing of, 280
Tokyo Rose
    European counterpart, 263
    identity, 262
Tom Collins (drink), 259
Tom Thumb, height, 258
Tony Awards, 169
Toothbrush, invention, 105
Tootsie Rolls, meaning of "Tootsie"
    in, 235
Tories, 282
Transatlantic flight, first, 76
Transportation to work, favorite
    mode, 20
Triangle Waist Company fire,
    number of deaths, 149
Triple Crown, multiple winner, 225
Trojan War, 277
Trotsky, Leon, 200
    birth name, 284
Troy
    location, 79
    size, 80
Truce of God, 281
Tucson, Arizona, bank robbery in,
    39
Tupperware, invention, 232
Turkey
    at first Thanksgiving, 1
    running speed, 23
"Twelve Days of Christmas," number
    of gifts in song, 92
12-tone theory (music), 67
23-Skiddoo (phrase), 49
Typewriter exercise, 111
Typhoid fever, 212
Typhoid Mary, reality of, 260
Typhus, 212

U.N.C.L.E. (United Network
    Command for Law and
    Enforcement), 168
Union of Soviet Socialist Republic
    (USSR), republics in, 87
Union Stock Yards (Chicago), 10

United Arab Emirates, 88
United Kingdom
    formation of, 82
    line of peerage, 197
United Nations
    number of sites, before move, 287
    secretary-generals, 287–288
United States
    Cabinet, first female to hold post
        in, 78
    capitals of each state, 180–182
    census, first, 5
    elevations, 22
    first born, of English settlers, 1
    first labor strike in, 5
    geographic center, 21
    hostages held in Iran, 14
    largest city in area, 18
    national debt increase in, 14
    natural attractions, most popular,
        16
    northernmost point, 21
    oldest hospital in, 2
    personal per-capita income, 17
    points in contiguous, farthest
        apart, 21
    population rank, 276
    right to tax, 11
    Senate, number of members in,
        174
    tallest building in, 17
    territories in Cuba, 88
    thirteen original colonies, 180
    visiting British royalty, first, 200
Upside down (phrase), origin, 61
Uranium, suppliers, 272
Used-car dealership, first, 74

Valhalla, location, 193
Vanity Fair, existence of, 142
Vatican City (Rome), 82
Vaudeville, derivation of word, 154
V-E Day, 286
Venice, doges, 197
Vesuvius, Mount, cities destroyed by
    eruption, 280
Vichy government, head of, 262
Victoria (queen of England), 198–
    199
    places named for, 89
Vietnam, last Americans to leave, 13
Vietnam War, Americans who died
    in, 13
Virtues, seven, 175

V-J Day, 286
Vote, right of women to, 283–284
Voter turnout
    age group, highest in U.S., 17
    presidential, 16, 17
Vowels, words that use all five, 62
Vulcan, existence of, 210

Wage(s)
    female vs. male, 19
    first minimum, 12
Waiting till the cows come home
    (phrase), 62
Wales, Prince of, creation of title,
    196–197
Walk around world, length of time
    to, 229
Washington, George
    birthday, 93
    inauguration money, 245
Water
    daily average use, 18
    fluoridated, 18
    freezing point, 210
    lifetime usage, 101
Wave, breaking of, 206
"We are all worms, but I do believe
    that I am a glowworm," 266
Wedding, head groomsman at, 51
Wedding rings, wearing of, 137
Weight, avoirdupois, 212
Westminster Abbey, interment at,
    275
Whale, ambergris in, 34
"Whenever I feel like exercise, I lie
    down until the feeling passes,"
    265
Whigs, 282
Whistler's Mother (painting), 66
White Hand Society, 37
"Who's on First" (comedy routine),
    complete lineup in, 160
Wilson, Woodrow, 248
Wind speeds, top five cities, 15
WIN (Whip Inflation Now) buttons,
    14
Witch hazel, origin of term, 120

Wizard of Oz, The, Dorothy's last
    name in, 159
Wolf, as symbol of troubles to be
    kept from door, 61
Women
    commemorated on U.S. postage
        stamp, first, 73
    earnings, vs. male earnings, 19
    first to win Pulitzer Prize for
        fiction, 129
    general in U.S. armed forces, first,
        73
    as head of political party, 78
    ordination of, in U.S. churches,
        190
    quoted in *Bartlett's Familiar
        Quotations*, 117
    representations on U.S. currency,
        7
    right to vote, 283–284
    in space, first, 78
    in U.S. Cabinet, first, 78
World leaders, nicknames, 195
World Series, winner of first, 221
Wuthering Heights (Bronte, Emily),
    173

Xanadu, location, 125
Xmas, 94–95

"Yankee Doodle" (song), 3
Yawning, longest recorded attack, 97
Yellowstone National Park
    (Wyoming), 16
Yin and yang, female half, 145
"You can never be too rich or too
    thin," 265

Zeus
    nine daughters, 140
    parents, 135
Ziegfeld girl, perfect, measurements,
    156–157
ZIP (Zoning Improvement Plan)
    code, 114
Zoo, first in U.S., 72
Zygote, gamete vs., 101